Sociological Foundation of Education

Srinibas Bhattacharya

ATLANTIC
PUBLISHERS & DISTRIBUTORS (P) LTD

ATLANTIC
PUBLISHERS & DISTRIBUTORS (P) LTD

7/22, Ansari Road, Darya Ganj, New Delhi
Tel.: +91-11-4077 5252, 2327 3880
E-mail: orders@atlanticbooks.com
Web: www.atlanticbooks.com

Published by Atlantic Publishers & Distributors (P) Ltd., 2002
Reprint 2006, 2008, 2022, 2024

Printed & bound in India by Atlantic Print Services

Preface

The *Sociological Foundation of Education* has added a new dimension to education as an inter-disciplinary approach.

Man not only lives in a society, he grows and functions in a social context and various factors contribute to the growth of an individual.

Sociology which involves the study of the society, social process and social change is a growing science.

Education can hardly be separated from society and so from Sociology.

School is a miniature society and what happens in a society also happens in a school situation.

The factors which are dealt with in a social context may be classified under human, environmental and organizational factors.

Like parents in a family, teachers take important roles in a school.

Culture occupies a significant place in a society.

A community cannot grow without culture. Similarly, a society cannot survive without culture. As in every dynamic society there are problems, so in every school there are typical situations.

Teacher has a distinct role as a social worker and community member.

Of all the foundations of education the sociological basis has a more practical bearing on day-to-day living.

Srinibas Bhattacharya

Contents

	Preface	*iii*
1.	Introduction	1
2.	What is Society?	6
3.	Society and Environment	15
4.	Culture	26
5.	Social Forces and Social Controls	34
6.	Social Stratification	42
7.	The Concept of Social Change	49
8.	The School and the Community	54
9.	The Present Scene in Indian Society	63
10.	An Analysis of Some of the Problems in India in Educational Perspectives	75
11.	New Perspectives in Education	96
12.	Education for Emancipation of Creative Consciousness and Inner Harmony	103
13.	Education for Peace	110
14.	Education for Harmony	115
15.	Education for Survival	119
16.	Education for International Understanding	128

1

Introduction

THE SOCIOLOGY OF EDUCATION

Education is an activity which goes on in a society, and it's aims and methods depend on the nature of the society in which it takes place. Education is a means of organizing the individual self and the social self into a disciplined stable and a meaningful unity. Mannheim on the other hand does not regard education solely as a means of realizing abstract ideals of culture. According to him, education can only be understood when we know for what society and for what social position the pupils are being educated.

Sociology is the study of society. The chief concern of sociology is the social relationships of mankind. Thus, it includes topics like social structure and organization, the interaction of social groups and the means of social control.

Thus, sociology of education studies the relations between education and society.

It is obvious that the study of educational sociology can make a valuable contribution both to sociology and to society.

The separate use of two terms educational sociology and sociology of Education might be maintained in order to preserve the distinction between the two types of emphasis, *viz.*, one upon the sociological problems — their bearing on education and the other on the educational problems with their bearing on sociology.

Educational sociology is the study of the interaction of the individuals and cultural environment which includes other individuals' social groups and patterns of behaviour. It is the science which describes and explains the institutions, social groups and the social processes.

As sociology contributes to education, education offers sociology the direction toward progress through experimentation. The system of education provides situation in which experiments are possible without offending values about human beings. The sociology of education is thus an analysis of the sociological processes involved in the educational institution. The right approach emphasizes the need for studying the group-processes and social interaction within the educational institution.

Karl Mannheim has outlined three courses for inclusion in the teacher-training programme as follows:

(a) Sociology for the educator,

(b) The sociology of education, and

(c) The sociology of teaching.

While sociology of education is mainly concerned with the study of the social phenomena within the school for improving the social climate and social life of the institution, educational sociology has its main task of using education as a social control. It aims at applying the sociological principles to the administration and process of education, as it is concerned with shaping the child's behaviour in the light of the community need. It describes the group process to which individuals are subjected and the influence of one group upon another to provide an understanding of the context within which the aims of education are pursued.

In other words, sociology builds upon the knowledge of many fields and relates it to the social environment.

SOCIOLOGICAL FOUNDATION OF EDUCATION

Sociologists regard education as a distinctively social phenomenon. Thus, a sociological perspective of education is important. While sociologists are primarily concerned with building a body of verified knowledge about education in social context, they are also concerned with the problem of applying their findings and conclusions in the field of education. Thus education needs a sociological foundation for its meaningfulness in social contexts.

A number of sociologists used to think of educational sociology as a field which would offer clues to the solution of social problems. In fact, education was looked upon as a process involving the function of improving society. The works of Good[1], Ellwood[2] and others[3] lay emphasis on education as the means to progress in society. They expressed the ideal that school might succeed in teaching the pupil to exercise social control for ensuring promotion of culture. Another concept of educational sociology was developed in the social perspective of education and it was hoped that it would help in determining the social objectives of education. Thus an attempt was made to arrive at a social philosophy of education to be based on an analysis of society and the needs of people in society.

Educational sociology has been defined as the application of sociology to educational problems. Brown said in this connection that "The educational sociologists utilize all that has been learnt in both the fields and adds them to a new science by applying sociological principles to the whole process of education."[4] He also adds that it is particularly interested in finding out how to manipulate the educational process to achieve better personality development.

While educational sociology was looking for its popularity because of its confusing nature of content, sociology of education has emerged as more relevant a subject for prospective teachers. In recent years, greater interest has been shown in the analysis of the educational system as a pattern of social interaction and thus a different role for sociology in relation to education has been conceived. Emphasis is being laid on the nature of human

1. Alvin, "*Sociology and Education*," Harpers, 26 (1926), p. 25.
2. Ellwood, C.A., "*What is Educational Sociology*?" Journal of Educational Sociology (September 1927), pp. 25-30.
3. Kinneman John A., "*Society and Education*" New York, Macmillan, 1932, p. 49.
4. Brown Francis. *Educational Sociology*, Prentice-Hall, New York, 1947.

relations within the school and the social structure within which the schools operate in the community. The patterns of interaction in the educational system are, therefore, receiving greater attention.

Education means different things to different people. It is a process as well as a product. Thus it has a definite role in the society. It is no wonder that education means something very important to a sociologist. Educational sociology is particularly interested in finding out, how to manipulate the educational process to achieve better social and personality development.

Educational sociology is interested in social behaviour as it includes anything in the field of sociology which could be related to the learning or socializing process. According to Brown, the educational sociologist not only utilizes all that has been learnt in both the fields, he also joins them in a new science by applying sociological principles to the entire process of education. It is also viewed that educational sociology is more a technology than a science. According to Dodson, "Educational sociology is interested in the impact of the total cultural milieu in which and through which experiences are acquired and organized." Educational sociology today lays emphasis on the analysis of the role of education in the community and society.

SOCIOLOGY OF EDUCATION AND SOCIAL FOUNDATION OF EDUCATION

In short, sociology of education is the scientific study of the social processes and social patterns involved in the educational system. This assumes that education is a combination of social acts which deals with analysis of human interaction. Education draws attention from a sociological point of view. Thus in the sociology of education emphasis is laid on education in relation to social perspectives. The social interaction and socialization within the school and community gains prominence in the sociology of education.

1. Educational sociology has been considered as an area which would provide the basis for social progress and social change.
2. Educational sociology is also supposed to provide specific aims for education.

3. Educational sociology deals with the entire process of socialising a child. It aims to study the patterns of social interaction and Social roles within the school and society. Thus a scientific study of the human relations in education is one of the objectives of sociology of education. It also deals with the social processes and patterns involved in the educational system.

   Sociology also deals with:

(a) The relationship of the educational system to the process of social and cultural change.

(b) The functions of the educational system in the process of social control.

(c) The relationship of education to the social class of status system.

(d) The relationship between the school and the community.

Thus, the need for a comprehensive study of the human relations in the educational system is receiving more and more attention in recent times.

With the rapid expansion of social science, sociology has included a vast area of social phenomena.

2

What is Society?

Introduction

Society is an enduring group of living beings carrying on all their activities in common. It is a dynamic body consisting of a large number of people under the same basic circumstances. It is just like a complex web of relations and various forces and factors go into its making. In a society, therefore, there exists a common ideal or belief, some mutual understanding and a common frame of reference.

Society is the creation of man. It is one of the monumental achievements of human beings. It is something more than a multitude of people as it contains different bodies but one mind, manifold expressions but one ideal.

Same basic factors of society: There are certain basic factors which comprise society. They act and interact and operate in a sort of dynamic equilibrium. These factors provide for the growth of society and social life. Population is the set of people, who build up the society. In course of living together these people undergo a process of adjustment to the environment. Natural environment including contour, rivers, seas, deserts, mountains and plains is another important factor comprising society. The people comprise the dynamic forces which operate in a particular field, *i.e.*, environment. Besides, there are resources, *viz.*, minerals vegetation, animals and the like which play their part and contribute to the development of society. Man meets his basic needs by getting suitable food, clothing dwelling and other amenities of life by dint of continuous efforts. Much depends upon environment. The habits are also influenced by environmental factors. Different lands represent the world communities. They build up definite patterns of living, culture and taboos according to the local conditions.

The physical environment sometimes provides man's physical needs and sometimes hinders the growth. The occupation and the living conditions are often guided by this geographical factor. It will be observed that people living in deserts are often restless and rootless and nomadism is the normal mode of their life. On the other hand, rivers foster in man a centralising tendency. According to Gidding, some degree of total aggregation is an indispensable condition for the evolution of society. This is known as a population which may vary in kind and density. Population, though one of the important factors of a society, is not all. Location has got a large part to play. The local conditions vary to a great extent and lead to diversity. It is location which offers clue to adjustment.

With the changing time man is changing in interaction with his local needs and conditions. Localisation of industry is one of the most recent trends in sociology and this is nothing but natural. Besides population and location, communication deserves special emotion. This is one of the important means for mobilising resources according to human needs. It is a wide term which may convey the various ways of social intercourse and transport. This is an attempt to adjust and bring a dynamic life. Today when living has become complex and needs increased, our world has become too small. Communication is being speeded up in order to keep pace with the changing time. Social structure changes but there remain sudden fundamental character in every society and social order. It is human nature which works as the dynamic force in every community.

In the present society man is trying his best to conquer nature and to dominate over the various forces. But how far he will succeed, will depend upon his know-how to bring harmony between man and the machine.

Family

A family is a place where the child grows and unfolds its potentialities. In other words, much depends upon the family stimulation, love and affection within the family. The mutual trust, respect and cordiality among fellow beings, in the social environment shape the personality of the family members. In India when fellow-feeling and humanitarian outlook were held in high esteem, family life was more integrated and conducive. Everyone enjoyed the joint family system where they could share their joy and sorrow. All the members used to live together in the same family in peace and happiness. Mutual trust and tolerance formed the basis of altruistic motive. So Indian culture was that of mutual co-operation and love, giving rise to a humanitarian outlook. With the growing impact of western culture on our society we have become more self-centred and less tolerant. The economic factors are, no doubt, responsible for such a change but there are other forces which are equally responsible for this difference in outlook. As a result, the Indian culture is under conquest gradually giving way to the foreign influence in changed circumstances. On an analysis it will be seen that a large number of factors have to be considered for forming a proper estimate of a culture.

The following is the list of such factors:

1. Miscellaneous factors including income, occupation, education, language, habits, type of residence, spending habit, etc.
2. Lifestyles, clothes and dress, eating and diet, physical habits and means of keeping health, attitudes to marriage and sex, techniques of bringing up children and patterns of family life.
3. Leisure pursuits—reading, radio and television programmes, sports, entertainment, means of artistic expression, etc.
4. Beliefs and value systems, moral attitudes and standards, religious beliefs, political views, social ambitions and aims in life.

The modern family is a group of interacting personalities in which each member has a specific role. Family is an important unit in the society because the child's personality and its development depend to a great extent upon its size and organisation. Today with the changing society the patterns of family life in India are also changing. The interaction between one member and another, the obligation and responsibilities assumed in family today are not the same as in the past.

The family patterns change from place to place and depend upon customs, standards and ideals, folk-ways and culture of society. Family is an expression of the richest fulfillment of human need among people of every race and nation. It is as old as man himself. Society and school should go hand in hand preparing healthy citizens. Democracy in education has carried a message of hope and goodwill and admitted of the equality of human rights and opportunities. But this is a concept very difficult to be translated into action. In spite of the best attempt to remove disharmonies there are disappointing pictures everywhere in our country. Even now, education is a luxury to many, who exhaust all their energies and time for making their both ends meet. Besides the conditions of our schools are in majority deplorable. There is hardly any parent-teacher co-operation, and scope for recreation and relaxation on the part of the children. It is, therefore, natural that our educational programme does often fail to create interests among children. Joy and freedom are only to be found in the dictionary. Particularly in the urban schools there is no breathing space for the children.

The inter-relation between society, philosophy and educational theory

Before going to show the inter-relation between society, state and philosophy in education, it would be worthwhile to describe the social implication of education. The significance of the social dimension of educational philosophy varies according to conception of how individuals should be related to each other. Some societies notably those in democratic state recognise the differences among individuals. It may also be wise to narrate the nature of society itself. Since society is contractual it would not be unfair to think that it goes as a result of mutual interaction between individual and social interest. Education, according to Bertrand Russell, has much to contribute to the welfare of society. Here education has an independent role to play. Similarly, society is one of the important agencies influencing educational activities. Education has a close relationship to society as they interact on one another. As society is guided by educational ideas, so education is influenced by the social forces. Education as a social control has the power to bring the necessary changes which are deemed desirable from time to time. Like society, state has also certain influence on the educational programme. State as a social control is far more effective than any other factor of society and is thus in a position to bring new impacts. Some time, the needs of the state are to be fulfilled through education which can foster a spirit of nationality in the young generation of the country. Thus society, state and education are interlinked as they have got the same objectives, namely, the happiness of man. For the promotion of international understanding education may be profitably employed and the world citizenship may be rendered feasible. The question then arises as to the importance of philosophy in the sphere of education. It has been already admitted that society has the highest role as it represents the people and their culture. The taboos and customs are sometimes modified according to the changing attitude of people towards life. It is admitted on all hands that education is also conditioned by economic factors. At the same time one can hardly ignore the influence of philosophy on our daily life and education. In our discussion on educational values, it must be remembered that philosophy is also reflected upon the educational principles or policy. For example, the democracy in education has brought a new era in the world of education by pronouncing the principle of equality of opportunity. This principle of democracy has, no doubt, been inspired by the philosophy underlying humanitarian outlook. It asserts that every individual should be treated as an end. The concept of freedom and joy in the field of education is also another outcome of this new outlook. The rigid and traditional view-point has been replaced by this new concept as propagated by the modern thinkers in this field. In short, education is an active process which functions in a most dynamic manner for better adjustment in the interest of the common cause. Today education has gained a distinctive status of its own because of its high potential.

FACTORS INFLUENCING EDUCATION

The Concept of Social Role

A person learns to behave in his cultural group and develops in a society. The roles depend on the different statuses he occupies as he grows up. Some roles are of a special kind which a community assigns to all its members. Another type of status is achieved by the efforts of the individual, who reaches a position in his group. The social group thus helps in setting up a general standard of behaviour expected by the community as a whole. It should be mentioned in this connection that appropriate forms of behaviour are also laid down to suit different social occasions and the individual response according to situation. The concept of social role can also be extended to group membership of all kinds. As the social interaction increases, the child begins to learn his role in different groups and to absorb the varied patterns of behaviour. His prestige and success in the group will depend upon the group values. The wishes and attitude of the group are impressed upon the child by the degree of approval and disapproval of his actions. Each group will have its various techniques for maintaining discipline. It is sufficient to point out that the approval of the group is one of the strongest incentives to right behaviour. The child who will not fit into any group develops some more or less serious problems or disturbance in personality. The child learns the ways of his society along with any desire to change them by the growing concept of his role in social groups. The groups to which he can give his full loyalty and in which he achieves status through his efforts are of great significance to his development. Whatever may be the group formation, some social learning of the following kinds can be observed to take place: (1) The struggle for leadership and the shifting nature of this role. (2) The need for roles and training the individual wishes for the good of the group (3) The expression of the child's needs for some emotional response from his playmates. (4) The need to belong to a group and the struggle to be accepted by the group. (5) The opportunity given for co-operation and learning the team spirit. (6) The first experience of inter-group opposition or a rivalry by the other groups and possibly a conflict with the family over codes of behaviour learnt from the group.

It is in adolescence that the need develops for more organised groups which are conventionalised and have a more permanent purpose and tradition. In whatever form it takes the value of social interaction to adolescence, the following are the needs which group life may be expected to satisfy. (1) The adolescent has a great need for a social group experience and to experiment new relationship with others of his own age. (2) Some such group experiences can take place in family, school or work groups and voluntary membership of a group of different kind may fulfill other needs. (3) The need to mix with members of opposite side or sex is not insignificant. (4) A group or club of which a boy chooses to be a member may also be run by the member. (5) As a part of the group a young person learns to accept responsibility. (6) The adolescent needs for adventure are of a legitimate kind. (7) Adolescent learns a great deal from each other. The function of youth in society has been considered from a sociological point of view and co-operation of a youth in a changing and dynamic society has been regarded as very important.

Social Interaction in the School

A school carries on an organised life of its own as a social group within the society around it. A school is some time referred to as a society but it would be better if we call this a community since its members have many things in common. The school as a society makes the following definite suggestions which are summarised as follows: (1) That pupils themselves should take some share in making the school's programme. (2) That a greater number of pupils should take responsibility. (3) Minor organisations should be left to the pupils. (4) There should be closer relation between the school and the society outside. Thus a school should stimulate a healthy social life and promote the social understanding.

The social interaction is influenced also by family life which is the first and the most intimate group to which the child belongs. We are concerned with nature of the family as a social unit. The functions of the family have been classified in various ways as follows: (1) In giving and receiving affection, the value of the family circle as a source of love and security cannot be over emphasised. This continues to be a major function of home life. (2) As the function of proper reproduction a family unit must adjust the birth of children. The size of the family has a considerable influence upon society. (3) The family known as the unit of production has to supply its own needs. Agencies outside the home have gradually taken over more and more economic function. (4) The family used to take full responsibility for protecting its members. Now, the state has taken much of the responsibilities. The family still gives the protection or affection which leads to the kind of emotional security which cannot so far be acquired in any other way. (5) Education is also being taken over more and more by the state. The tendency has been to raise the school leaving age at one end and the lower age of entry at the other. (6) Recreation and relaxation which the home used to provide are the chief sources of leisure and stimulation in occupation. Children and parents spend less of their leisure time at home. The sport, the case of transport, the outdoor activities, the desire to travel, the independence of women have all contributed to this change. The cinema takes people out but these have limited effect. (7) Each member in the family has a clearly defined status and each status has its role. Thus human relations within a family are very important.

Parent-teacher Relation

The family life of a pupil is also stimulated by the parent-teacher relation. Since the school is tending to share the function of the family, it is necessary to provide frequent opportunities for contacts between parents and teachers.

Outside Cultural Influences

As discussed previously, the influence of group membership in transmitting the culture of our society is remarkable. The most important source of influences (external to the small group) is the mass-medium of communication. This consists of cinema, the radio, newspapers and magazines. All these are medium of communication in an industrial society in which we live. All the features of our life and the interests of people are being brought to public notice through these mass-media of communication. The printed word has influenced on the mind and the impact of the modern printing press on universal literacy is great. The influence of cinema on the children leads to dissemination of cultural values and habits. Thus with the changing time our culture is also being influenced by the various scientific innovations and attitudes of the people. The social role is, therefore, an important concept where the various institutions like school and club, family and church, cinema and press, interact and shape the future generation.

Culture Concept and Social Institutions

As defined by Ralph Linton, a culture is the organisation of learned behaviour and the result of behaviour whose component elements are shared and transmitted by the members of a particular society. A culture pattern can be taken to mean the ways of behaviour associated with any permanent need or function in the social life. It is also represented by material objects which are included under the results of behaviour.

3

Society and Environment

SOCIAL FACTORS AND SOCIAL ORGANISATION

Environment provides the basis for the growth or social development as society is formed as a result of interaction within a geographical boundary. Population is one of the factors of the society although its size, structure and organisation vary to a considerable extent. Environment influences people in a number of ways. There may be different types of physical environment, social environment and cultural environment. The climate, natural resources, the nature of the soil influence, the distribution of population, the food habit and even the habitat chosen by people. Besides, the type of surface of the land has a bearing on the personality of the people in respective areas. For example, people living in hill areas are more painstaking than those on the plains. Similarly, those living in islands are more outgoing and courageous than others. Thus the nature of the physical environment has a distinct bearing on the body and mind, the habit and personality of people. Even population is distributed differently according to the physical environment, industrial growth and natural resources.

Like physical environment, social and cultural environment also determine the attitude and outlook of the people in a society. Certain communities are socially backward because of their inability to accommodate new ideas and values. Exposure to the outside world and varieties of culture leads to broadness of outlook. It is interesting to observe that certain communities are very rigid and conservative while there are communities with greater adaptability. It may be relevant in this connection to mention that certain monuments of civilization have been built-up on the banks of the rivers like the Ganges and the Nile. Thus the contribution of river to the growth of culture and civilization and the Egyptian culture are examples, no doubt.

In addition to physical environment, certain other factors are related to the development of a society. Among them the cohesion and morale, the nature of interaction between members of society, the values, common faith and belief deserve special mention. In order to bring a cohesive pattern of community-life certain goals and common ideology would be essential. In addition to the physical or geographical factor the interaction among the members of the society determines the pattern of the social structure of a society. Of course communication and culture help the process of social interaction. Thus among the factors of society, cultural values and norms, interaction and means of communication play prominent roles. Besides, the social units and social groups form the internal structure and generate the forces.

Needless to mention, that social environment is created as a result of interplay between the people and the socio-cultural factors. This kind of environment contributes to the growth and development of a society. The last but not the least important type of environment is the cultural environment, as it provides the guideline for formation of values and norms in a social context. The richer the cultural environment, the more conducive it becomes to the growth of personality. A civilisation is enriched by the affluent cultural environment for obvious reasons.

Factors of Society

Society is like a complex wave of relationship between various groups of people. There are certain factors which comprise a society. A geographical boundary, within which people live in interaction with one another, is essential for a stable society to build up. But more important factor is population or a set of people with common interests or goals. Even a natural environment including rivers, sea, deserts influence the social structure and the social function. The composition of the social classes and the distribution of population depend mainly upon the available natural resources as well as transportation system. Communication media serve the purpose of interaction at various levels. Thus the entire social fabric is the outcome of so many threads running into one another for adequate functioning.

In addition, there are social units around which the social activities are continued for the promotion of the set objectives. Of all the units family deserves special mention because of its vital importance. Family is a place for socialization where the child grows in a sheltered situation. It provides a background for transfusion of social values. In fact, the role of family in a child's development is quite significant. There are other social units which go to the making of a society. They are religious institutions, social organisations like club, educational centres including schools and similar social units.

The factors mentioned above, no doubt, condition education as they influence the growth and distribution of population, social mobility and social structure. Even the social stratification depends upon the economic status of people as well as their educational achievements. It is interesting to find out relationship between the growth of as well as the cultural decline. In a changing society the media of communication play an important role in bringing social change or social progress.

The social forces are the result of social interaction. They produce social changes as well as create conditions for social progress. Among the social units certain sub-structures develop more communication channels and individual values. Social classes including castes are the outcome of the economic and cultural disparities found in a social structure. They create conflicts and dissatisfaction within the unprivileged section because of the stratification. In certain tribes or sections of the society we find less mobility and more rigidity. Even today most of the aboriginal tribes tend to cling to the old values and resent any change even in a desired direction. For example the depressed classes in India were very reluctant to accept the value of family planning and population control. Similarly, among the American Indians there still exists some resentment against modern technical education. With a view to generating public opinion and new values the roles of mass-media and recreational agencies are tremendous. The social organisations, economic and industrial institutions can contribute substantially to the cause of mass enlightenment and national integration.

The Individual and Social Organisation

The social relations are developed by the way people behave with each other and by their membership in groups. There are many ways in which an individual interacts, sometimes through co-operation and at other times through competition and conflict. It is observed that interaction follows an established pattern. The individual's interaction and his group memberships are mainly determined by the way in which he solves the problem of day-to-day life. There is a variety of social relations built up through friendship, leadership, partnership, citizenship and host of other relations. Some social bonds are strong while others are delicate. Marriage remains a relatively strong and stable bond. Moreover, the strength of a relation depends on whether it serves the needs of the individual.

The social structure consists of a number of roles defined as patterns of behaviour associated with a distinctive social position, *e.g.*, that of father, teacher, employer, etc. The ideal role, however, prescribes the rights and duties belonging to a social position. Most roles are more complex than they appear to be. Yet it is necessary to specify the social position with which it is associated, as the individual is subject to conflicting pressure and strain in course of his functioning. Some of these strains arise as a natural consequence. The role conflicts may be observed in various areas in industry and military life and so in education. The individual gains much from his involvement in social organisation. There are many types of group interactions which determine a particular social group. In fact, mere assemblies of people without interaction do not constitute groups which differ greatly in character, purpose, mood and cohesiveness. Some groups last longer, while others are relatively momentary. For example, the most enduring group is the kinship group which involves only the immediate blood-relations. Similarly there are territorial groups formed on the basis of their residence and interaction. Thus community is a large unit while neighbourhood is a group of common locality whose members share not only the feelings but also the advantages and disadvantages. Like territorial groups there may be interest groups which are formed on the basis of common interest. There are other classifications on the basis of the nature of relationship. They are primary and secondary groups. The intimate groups are face-to-face groups which are enduring. The family is an example of the primary group as it is very close and intimate as a social unit.

Secondary groups are impersonal groups where relationships are less enduring. However, many groups fall between the ideal primary groups and the extreme secondary groups.

Thus not all small groups are primary as the primary relations among the people, living and working together, form the criteria. On the other hand, primary groups can be formed in spite of the largeness of the size of the population forming the group. In short, a high degree of cohesion under sense of unlimited commitment may form a primary community. It is interesting that the nature of interaction varies from group to group. Love, friendship and intimate relations grow in a congenial setting fostering a close relationship among the members. In this connection it should be mentioned that primary relations are not necessarily good at all times. What is more important is the personal satisfaction derived from the interaction and a feeling of belongingness. Particularly during adolescence when the child faces a life of storm and stress, the need for socialization is almost imperative. He has to develop the coping mechanism within himself to face the hard realities of life in day-to-day struggle. The child has to learn to live with problems, deprivation and depressions in the hope of overcoming them. Socialization offers the key to living in conformity with the social demands as well as ethical standards. Unfortunately, education today is pre-occupied more with catering information than with the development of intrinsic qualities of head and heart. If we expect our new generation to take the responsibility and leadership in future society tomorrow, adequate preparation should be planned through educational activities accordingly.

The Family and Education

The family is one of the most important units in a social fabric. It is concerned with face to face relationship within the primary group it belongs to.

Edward Weztermorck held that the family was not necessarily rooted in marriage and that marriage is not an institution arising out of the family. There are two main types of family, *viz.*, the extended family and nuclear family.

In short, the family is the world's oldest and most basic social institution and can be considered as either a social institution or as a social group. As a social institution the family is a system of norms guiding interaction among persons related by blood or marriage. As a group, a family refers to relatives under one roof. In short, the concept of the family as a social institution is a sociological concept that focusses on norms rather than people.

Functions of the Family

Recently, responsibilities have been shared by many other social institutions. Family has still retained its two major functions: (a) Producing, and (b) Socialising children.

The family also performs the functions of regulating sexual behaviour, determining social class and providing emotional support and affection. Among the functions of the family, socialization of children deserves special mention. The child learns cultural patterns acceptable to the society. Socialization is the cumulative result of experiences. The child learns to participate in a society by observation.

The actual functions of the family enumerated by Murdock are mainly sexual, economic and educational. In fact, sexual family is a special agency for providing the affection to ensure the emotional stability and security so much needed for a happy and successful living. According to Talcott Parsons human personality is made through the socializing process promoted by families. Both father and mother have distinctive role and instrumental functions. While the father helps in establishing instrumentally the desired relations to external goal objects, the question of the expressive affairs of the family system and the integrative relations among its various members, remains pertinent.

Thus family is an institution which permits safeguarding the interest of the child during its period of biological immaturity, Socialization and initial education, are the means.

The functions of the family are different. As described by Ogburn, the functions are mainly: (1) affectional, (2) economic, (3) educational, (4) recreational, and (5) religious. Becker also lists the following functions of the family: (1) production of population, (2) protection and care of the child, (3) socialisation and education of the child, (4) reaction, and (5) affectional interaction. From the above two lists of functions, it is obvious that family has got a close bearing on the life and education of a child. The role of the family in the social adjustment of a child is too great to be ignored. In the present society, family life in India is gradually losing integrity and harmony. This may be partly owing to economic factors. But there are many other factors responsible for the change in the family structure, *e.g.*, (1) marriage age and rate, (2) conflicts between the family members, (3) employment of the women, and (4) the encouragement of extreme individualism.

As days are passing the number of broken homes, divorces and separations are increasing even in our country. As a result, the child development is adversely affected. The spirit of tolerance and sacrifice is fading away and the smooth functioning of a family is also affected. With this family background, a child enters into school and faces problems of adjustment. He cannot see things and conditions favourable for his social and intellectual growth. This is one of the main problems leading to the problem of backwardness and juvenile delinquency.

The School

Education takes a significant role in every human society and the school has a unique function to carry out. It is school which can transmit effectively the cultural heritage from generation to generation. So the school has a significant role and responsibility.

The School as a Social Institution

Education takes place in all human societies. The school concept has developed eventually as a social institution for transmission of cultural patterns and cultural heritage. In fact, the school has a greater impact on community life because of its direct involvement with culture. It is a major force in shaping the cultural pattern according to be needs of the community. As a social institution it helps the process of socialization by fostering the social values. The school not only creates a favourable situation for interaction among individual members school is a miniature society. It also generates a climate for the development of in-group and inter-group relations. In the words of Ruth Strong, "The social cosmos of the school is the children's own world. The processes of affiliation, identification, group action and interaction are among the primary means of social development for all children."

The teacher is the most important person in determining the extent to which the in-group feeling is developed. He can create a learning situation where the students roles and participation contribute to the development of social awareness within the groups. Thus the dynamics of human relations find their expression in a variety of social situations. The teacher is the key person to lead his pupil into active membership in a fraternity to which he himself belongs. He is, thus, in a position to serve as an important link between the community as well as the school. Nevertheless the role of the teacher is not as easy one as it involves a number of difficult functions. In the words of Alexander. "The calling of a teacher, as so defined, is one of infinite difficulty. But it is also infinitely significant. He is commissioned to form and fashion both human society as a whole and the individuals of whom that society consists."

Socialization

Socialization is a process which continues for the entire life-span of an individual. It is the way, culture is transmitted as it humanises the biological organism by regulating behaviour. At different stages of human life different modes of socialization are observed. An infant grows as he interacts with the environment for enrichment of his biological existence. Socialization is the outcome of man's adjustment to his social environment. It inculcates basic disciplines and produces a degree of conformity. It also instills aspirations and teaches social values and their supporting traits. Socialization may be the product of spontaneous human interaction or it may be deliberate and planned. An individual is socialized by a number of agencies including the family and school.

Socializing the child is a must for his development. The social response of the parents is based upon needs and values already formed in a particular culture and society. It goes without saying that socialization helps to create a self-image and an ego.

In conclusion, one may say that socialization and education are not different. Both involve life-long process. They take place at various stages of human development. Socialization of the child is no less important. The child's father presents as authority figure particularly in Indian families and takes the role of the captain of the ship. While a child grows he becomes aware of his expected norm of behaviour. He learns to comply and conform to the norms set by the family community and society. Besides, it is important to have acceptance, respect and appreciation for the development of personality. Giving and receiving love help socialization. Similarly reward and punishment, praise and reprimand contribute to the process of socialization. All the members of the family, play-groups as well as associates have significant roles in the child's socialization.

The school environment is, no doubt, a source of socialization of the child as it inevitably produces a degree of conformity through discipline, reward and punishment. The teachers serve as agents to effect this process of socialization while the pupils interact and develop values of their own. The classroom provides learning situation promoting socialization through mutual help and co-operation competition and conflict. Similarly the co-curricular activities organised in the school contribute a lot toward the child's maturation and growth in terms of socialization. In fact, the child emerges as a social being and learns to step into new world of friends and associates, teachers and other members of the school community. In short, the push and pull, the plus and minus, confronted by a child in a school climate provide a strong foundation for social development. The child in course of his growth receives stimulation from his environment in his own way. Thus school environment socializes children by its control and discipline, its nourishment and nurture. The child learns to react to the people around him appropriately and grows emotionally as well as socially. His parents help him to build up self-identity by giving love and affection and providing a basis of security. The father's role is significant in the process of building personal identity.

In the social context of modern India we find a dwindling or decaying relationship between members of the same social unit, *viz.*, family and other organisations. The sociologist and the educationist should see that the relationship between the members of the community is sustained.

Social Institutions

Social institution is the result of man's long endeavour to organise group-life. Any social system demands interaction among groups, and individuals and the social order. Among the social institutions the family deserves special mention, as it provides the shelter and a congenial climate for individual development. It gives a sense of belonging to life. Parents see the children taking up their role and responsibility for placing them in the life of the community. While a social institution provides a systematic way of meeting major group needs provided by culture, family serves as the cradle for nourishing individuals in the continuous process of adjustment. Patterns of family life differ widely although all the families have certain common roles as follows:

(a) Seeing a child reaching maturity,
(b) Socialising him in group-life, and
(c) Providing a cultural background to meet obligations for training.

The modern family is more than a number of persons living in one house-hold unit. It is a group of interacting personalities in which each member has a definite although varying role. These roles are never static as they change both with different situations and with different culture. Thus in a family the in-depth personal experience and the interaction between members create a bondage or familial cluster. The family as an institution assumed certain responsibilities enforced by community, but today those roles and responsibilities have become more formalised. Basically, the family doesn't depend upon legal sanction; it lies deep within the customs, standards and ideals — the folk-ways and mores of society. In short, the family is an expression of the maximum fulfillment of human need among people of every community.

4

Culture

Concept of Culture

Every society has its own culture or social heritage. It has been used with various meanings. The concept of culture was discovered recently as its significance has been realised more than ever. Culture has been defined by E.B. Taylor,[1] the English anthropologist, as "that complex whole which included knowledge, belief, art, morale, law, custom and any other capabilities and habits acquired by man as a member of the society." The concept originated with anthropologists but has been later on developed further in many other ways. As commonly used in the social science, culture refers to a social heritage. It is the distinctive way of life of a group of people and their complete design for living.

Thus, the idea of culture has a rich intellectual background as it refers mainly to ideals of enlightenment and refinement. This humanistic view of culture emphasises creativity and excellence. "It is transmitted socially by communication and gradually embodied in a group tradition of which the vehicle is language." Thus, the definition, given by Ellwood[2] is more specific. The idea of culture is used in the perspective of the entire society including aesthetic and moral attainments.

---

1. Taylor, E. B., *Primitive Culture*, page 1, Brentanas, 1924, N.Y.
2. Ellwood Charles, A., *Culture and Evolution*, page 9, New York, D. Appleton Century Company, 1927.

Anthropologists of the nineteenth century used culture and civilisation almost in the same sense. A line of demarcation was gradually discovered. The term 'civilisation' retained its evaluative connotation while culture referred to the total way of life of people in general.

A few observations on culture may be relevant at this point:

(a) Culture is free of value-judgments. It is mainly descriptive.

(b) The social influences on human nature and human achievement are projected in culture.

Thus, it includes ways of living in different contexts and the entire range of human activity. Anthropology emphasises a comprehensive view of culture instead of differences and distinctions. It assumed that humanity may be achieved through any sustained social experience. Culture has also been viewed more as a symbol in the realm of values. For the purpose of understanding culture two types of symbols should be taken into account. They are referential and expressive. The expressive symbols have a special significance for culture as they are connotative while the referential symbols are just words or objects having specific reference.

Culture is a design, the composite of guiding values and ideals. Hence, it is not difficult to discover the interdependence between culture and social organisation.

There are mainly two forms of culture. One is the material, while the other is non-material. The material culture consists of the tangible forms such as dress or any object that man has created for his own use. The development of art, new amenities and gadgets indicate the cultural progress of people. Thus the material aspect of culture includes cultural instruments.

The non-material culture is another form which is intangible but has a greater impact. This is noticed in, beliefs, attitudes and behaviour pattern in a society. Thus culture tends to be pervasive touching every aspect of life. It includes social activities and involves institutions. Like an individual a culture comprises a consistent pattern of thought and action, within each culture there may be sub-cultures. People living under one culture area will be similar in many respects. In India as well as in the United States there are many ethnic sub-cultures. The ethnic groups tend to be unique by their difference in dress, food-habits, as well as languages. Some sociologists mention about youth sub-cultures. In fact, there are cultural uniformities and cultural variations and sociology is interested in seeking explanations for those. In recent years there has been a great deal of interest in the study of cultural similarities and cross-cultural traits. The cross-cultural index is used by students and researchers in comparing the ways of life of people in various cultures. It is interesting to see that the cultures vary and at the same time they have something in common. Sociologists are intrigued by the problem of diversity in culture. Among the factors contributing to the variations: (a) Migration and isolation, (b) The geographical factor, and (c) Individual differences deserve special mention.

The study of the nature of culture reveals that culture is pervasive and at the same time cumulative. This is transmitted by teaching and learning. Thus the inter-relation of culture and the educative process is apparent.

The Impact of Culture

It is obvious that culture creates a world by providing a context within which individual inter-action takes place. Culture is an important determinant of thought and feeling. The impact of culture as a variable depends upon the particular aspect of culture involved and the related circumstances. People participating in culture in different degrees are more or less responsive to values and norms. Cultural norms are based on cultural values and they develop according to situation. There are rules that define appropriate and inappropriate ways of thinking. Mores are also rules for thinking, feeling and acting as they have moral significance. The folk-ways and mores are the routine ways of doing things developed through trial and error as people struggle to meet the needs of life. In other words, mores are those folk-ways identified with group-welfare and group-survival.

Sociologists use the term norms or cultural norms to include folk-ways and mores. In fact, a norm is a standard to guide and regulate proper and acceptable behaviour within the groups. Usually violation of norms, prescribed as a must, calls for some kind of punishment. These norms vary in degree of explicitness as some are spelled out very precisely while others remain flexible. It is interesting to study the components of culture and fit them into some classification-scheme. Clerk Wissler, a noted anthropologist, made such an attempt, but Wissler's outline was not comprehensive and elaborate. Education was excluded from his list, although he listed the major areas of socialisation.

It is culture which influences future developments. For practical purposes culture traits have been used in terms of culture complexes. Anthropologists, today, are interested at present in studying the culture-patterns like trait complexes. Thus the patterns of a culture are important for distinguishing one society from the other. Such patterns of culture are known as ethos.

In short, culture is a collective term for all behaviour patterns, socially acquired and socially transmitted. A recent definition of culture is that given in the book on Educational Sociology by Francis J. Brown, he defines culture as "the total behaviour pattern of the group conditioned in part by the physical environment both natural and man-made but primarily by the ideas, attitudes, values and habits which have been developed by the group to meet its needs."

Cultural Traits

Cultural trait is the simplest unit of culture. It may be material or non-material. Personality is shaped to fit into a culture. Similarly culture shapes us to fit into a particular way of life. It even moulds our ideas and beliefs concerning the world around life. Parts of a culture which everyone must learn are called cultural universal. Cultural specialties are parts of culture, while cultural alternatives are those aspects of culture in which one has a choice. As already mentioned, culture traits are combined into culture complexes. Like trait complexes and norms are inter-related to form culture patterns. The patterns of culture vary from area to area. For example, American culture patterns are different from oriental culture patterns. Like culture patterns there are culture areas over which a given type of culture prevails. Similarly there are ethnics of cultures and some other types of sub-cultures including occupational sub-culture.

In short, an inter-related chain is formed around central trait which is either an abstract or a concrete entity. This cluster of traits forms a culture complex. Thus, culture traits are not only inter-woven into larger patterns but are also characteristic behaviour patterns of constituent groups. The size of a culture area representing the portion of humanity depends upon the particular trait complex used as the basis of differentiation. There are many ways in which the cultural change takes place. Diffusion, acculturation and other methods are involved in the complex process of cultural change. Diffusion means the acceptance of cultural patterns from other groups while acculturation is a result of adaptation and eventual assimilation of one particular culture by a group.

Cultural Change

Cultural change takes place as a result of acculturation or diffusion. Acculturation is a term which is used as a synonym for socialisation. Like all cultural acquisitions, socialisation and acculturation are used almost in the same sense. Culture changes as a result of inventions or discoveries, industrialization or political revolution. Similarly, improvement in communication and transportation leads to cultural change. Any cultural change consists of the modification of existing material culture and the adoption of new patterns of behaviour. Thus the dynamics behind the cultural change need to be studied for the proper understanding of the process of cultural influx. Cultural changes are prompted by the dissatisfaction of people with the existing situation. Migration, war or conquest influence diffusion of culture. Diffusion may take place even without the deliberate attempt on any one's part.

A glance at the history will show that culture changes at crossroads at a particular point of time. For example, Egypt, Palestine and Arabia have undergone a dramatic cultural change in recent years. The factors which contribute to the diffusion of culture traits are as follows:

(a) Accessibility of communication and transportation;
(b) Migration, war and conquest;
(c) Prestige of the lending culture;
(d) Cultural preparedness of the recipients of culture;

(e) Utility of new elements in culture; and
(f) Appeal of new element.

Diffusion takes place with and without deliberate attempts. It becomes purposeful when diffusion is organised. Purposeful diffusion is ever on the increase as we are living in such an age when education and publicity need deliberate planning. For example, the United Nations as a special organisation, is seeking to defuse culture in a planned and purposeful way. In fact, this is the great age of purposeful diffusion.

It is obvious that social change and social evolution are not the same. Similarly cultural change does not necessarily occur through evolutionary process. Cultural change may be classified under three categories. Material culture changes fast. Culture evolves gradually. The evolutionary concept of social change is also undergoing change. It is now believed that a man is capable of defying the laws of evolutionary change. This is known as a telic process involving the intelligent and planned direction of natural and social forces toward the achievement of a purpose. The rate of social change is uneven and the variability of cultural change characterises different groups, *e.g.*, families, communities, etc. Variation in the rate of change also exists in different aspects of culture. For example, the material culture changes more rapidly than the non-material. It is observed that certain aspects of culture remain unchanged. In fact, modern culture has emerged after a lot of changes within the socio-cultural context. A rapid change in one part of the culture, however, requires re-adjustment in the various correlated parts of culture. This is known as the social or cultural lag which varies according to nature of the cultural material. It is desirable to minimise this cultural lag through adjustment. It is the unevenness of change in the forms of culture or lack of balance which is responsible for social problems. The task of education is to assist members of the society to face the cultural world realistically and to direct its development toward higher human goals.

Factors Resisting Change

There are certain factors that resist cultural change. They are negative as they impede the progress. The following deserve special mention:

(a) The overlapping of generation,
(b) Cultural inertia,
(c) Vested interests, and
(d) The degree of isolation.

Usually resistance to any change is the result of a fear of change. People get used to the existing state of things and show inertia. Similarly, any kind of vested interest including financial, personal or group benefit stands on the way to a desirable change. Besides, cultural isolation may be the result of close community, lack of outside contact or predjudice and bias. It is often experienced that the backwardness of a community persists because of the rigidity in outlook of its members, who are close minded and less amenable to change.

Changing Patterns in Family-life

It is interesting to observe the origin and development of the family in different contexts. The three aspects of the history of family have definite bearing on educational psychology. They are: (i) the child-parent relationship, (ii) the husband-wife relationship, and (iii) the shifts in the function of the family in its interactions with other community-groups.

In different cultures the child-parent relationship assumed different patterns according to the expectation of the community and family. Moreover, the belief and customs play a vital role in the area of treatment of the parent toward son and daughter or *vice-versa*. For example, in India a son is considered as a special gift of God. The line of dynasty is maintained and the father gains heaven. So in Indian context the sons gain prominence and more attention than the daughters.

It is also observed that certain cultures encourage the dominance of father and the whole family and the children are supposed to follow the dictations of the father without any question.

THE SCHOOL IN RELATION TO CULTURE

The modern world with its complex social structure and cultural heritage presents the fact that culture accumulates. The school generates education and culture. It transmits cultural heritage and develops values. The school reflects the culture of the community or the nation, but it is a major force in changing the cultural pattern.

The school reflects the culture of the community or the nation. It is a major force in changing the cultural pattern. The school provides the basis for extending the boundaries of understanding.

5

Social Forces and Social Controls

The Nature of Social Control

Social control is a collective term for those processes planned or unplanned, by which individuals are taught. Persuaded, or compelled to conform to the usages and life-values of groups, social control occurs when one group determines the behaviour of another group or when the group controls the conduct of its own members or where individuals influence the responses of other.

It operates at three levels:

(a) Group over group;

(b) Group over its members; and

(c) Individuals over their fellows.

In short, social control refers to the attempt to influence others in accordance with some previously developed ideal, goal or purpose.

The Development of the Concept of Social Control

Social control is both old and new as it also exerts in the most premature forms of human life.

The socio-cultural forms are of primary importance as they decide the direction in which social control operates.

Process in Social Control

Social control involves a complex social process underlying intricate social relationship. The analysis of social relationships and social orderliness may be approached in terms of what are called socio-psychic processes involving thought and feeling which arise in interactions among persons in organised group-life. All social controls are dependent upon communication which is fundamental to all social processes. There are various methods of communication including all the ways by which meaning is transferred from individual to individual.

While perception and experience play vital roles in the socio-psychic process in social control, mental set and the context in which experiences occur for the individual contribute to the entire process of social control.

Education as an Agent of Innovation

Social forces are the result of social interaction which is a process. This is mainly based on the different groups of associations and varying degree of inter-stimulations. The result is the evolution of different social controls. Personality is dynamic whereas environment is to be modified according to the needs of the changing time and society. Besides the individual action, there is a question of group mind and interaction. As a result, social customs and codes are framed not for individual interest but for the interest of a community. The interaction between individual and community interests sometimes leads to conflict. It is admitted that society consists of an aggregate of individuals' carrying on activities within a particular geographical area. This involves a system of relationship in which the activities of each individual supplement those of every other individual. This is essential for the functioning of a society as, it implies inter-dependence. Functional integration takes place with reference to the unity of a group or of society as a whole, as a result of a number of mutual and supplementary functions. In other words, the social roles that comprise a society are dependent on the various inter-group relations, Sociologists, however, recognise three bases of classification of the social interaction, *viz*., (a) In terms of the number of persons involved, (b) On the basis of degree of intimacy, and (c) Social processes of all these. The social processes will consist of adjustment, opposition and co-operation. These take place at various levels and a complex process of interaction goes on. Social interaction is, therefore, a multipolar process. It may take place between an individual and a group and between groups.

This concept of social interaction is of importance and is related to social force and social controls. There is mobility of population, impact of culture and other factors. These have given rise to a number of social forces. There are some, who believe that public opinion and religion are the two great social forces or controls having considerable influence upon society. The social forces are the product of man's volition and they contribute to group interaction. These forces are not the outcome of one or two individual directives as group mind has a large part to play in the formation of the social forces. When they become effective, they prove to be of importance as social controls. On an analysis it will be clear that the social controls can be enumerated as follows:

1. Education as a social control,
2. Religion as a social control, and
3. Public opinion as a social control.

Forms of Social Control

There are various forms of social control including non-violent means, *e.g.*, art, literature, religion and education.

Education as a Social Control: Education has assumed a great responsibility with the march of civilization. In the days of yore, when everything was in a state of flux, education was functioning mainly in the shape of instruction. It was more allied to preaching as in the field of religion, but it was realised that education should mean the spontaneous development of human virtues and potential. The task of education is to create opportunities for the enfoldment of those innate abilities and senility to the right, good and beautiful. It is through education that attitude can be changed and so the human behaviour. The modern thinkers believe in the autonomy of education. According to them, education should have an independent status irrespective of the individual needs and interests. It should have a reference to the fundamental and permanent value of life and thus should not be at the mercy of politics, or any other external pressure.

Every country today is confronted with the problems of stratification and disintegration. The basic instincts seek their outlet when no sufficient scope for their sublimation exists. Education should prepare the mind of the public for the right type of thinking and behaving in a society. It is essential because of the increasing tendency of mal-adjustment in every sphere of life. It should act both as an incentive as well as a control. The anti-social behaviour should be very carefully handled by means of proper education. The different social agencies should be well-organized, co-ordinated and properly motivated. This is possible only when education is granted sufficient freedom for its functioning. Education starts from the cradle and continues up to the end of life. It is a continuous process and is closely correlated to life itself. This is why education can easily sublimate the basic instincts and develop the healthy attitudes of the people at different stages of their lives. Through schooling, broadcasting, publicity, propaganda, press and other individual means, education can achieve its end and can prove as an effective social control.

Religion as a Social Control: Education first started from the church. The church had enough influence on people and public. It was the centre of cultural activities and religious instruction. Religion had a control over the society, but gradually the churchmen lost their hold because of their tendency towards propagating dogmas. Nevertheless, religion had its appeal because of its value in life. In spite of a good deal of conflicts between different religions, there are some fundamental values common to all.

Religion at first dominated over the feelings and as such it proved as a social control.

Religion can be described as the ethical code for adjusting human behaviour. It serves as a frame of reference for those, who find it difficult to adjust. This is why the role of religion is very prominent.

It is a major force in sustaining the cultural pattern of the group. It stimulates the highest aspirations of mankind and translates those into individual and community behaviour.

It tends to establish and perpetuate certain values within the total culture. In a majority of countries, state and church have influenced each other. One provided authority, and the other spiritual sanctions. The stability of the social order and the security of the state demand the religious solidarity of the people. It is a great force which acts on the mind of the people. As a social control, religion has hardly any parallel. The issue of religious instructions may bring conflict but every citizen would like to have one religion or other. It is a vital force in our culture and the school should have a regular programme of moral discourses. As a matter of fact, religion being an important part of culture forms an essential feature of life. There may be controversy about how religion can be used as a social control. It is a fact that in our daily life we cannot completely avoid religion so ingrained in our culture. By observing rites we conform to the dictation of religion. Religious sentiments prove very effective and strong, even for those who are not educated. It helps to form a group mind and guides human feeling and action. As such, religion should be regarded as one of the best social controls.

Law as a Social Control: The variation in state legislation and in judicial decision is great because of the circumstances. The difference among the states has to be taken into account. Law has a practical disciplinary value for obvious reasons. Man is not by nature always rational. He requires some dictation and guidance through legislation. It acts as a deterrent against tendency towards anti-social behaviour. There was a time when people used to decide their own fate and give out their opinion. But now-a-days it is not so forceful unless it is put in a very organised way. With the rising democracy public has been much conscious of their rights and individual judgment. So their opinion cannot be completely ignored. There have been cases when people have been more afraid of public opinion than of law or state.

India today is passing through a transition period and there have been conflicting views on the right principle to be adopted in various fields. Unfortunately enough, public opinion has not been fully organised at this stage because of the want of proper education among mass. So there is a danger in depending too much upon public opinion as a social control. Nevertheless, its influence will be there. With the growing individual consciousness people feel great difficulty in adjusting themselves to the state ideology at all times. They try to give vent to their feelings, thoughts and desires. For this, there is often a state of conflict at different levels of the society and public opinion has got its limitation. Besides these social controls, there are other forces working as controlling agents. For example, films, radios, advertisement and folklores have their influence on the mind of the people. They, therefore, can be used as social controls.

Public Opinion as a Social Control: Although the term 'public opinion' is a coinage of the late 18th century, a number of approximate equivalents may be traced to much earlier periods.

The struggles of 17th century England represent the step in clarifying the nature of function of public opinion. In the absence of a carefully set convention a great deal may pass as public opinion which in reality is merely the publicly expressed opinion of an individual or a small group, and is thus essentially personal in character.

Public opinion today is a great social control which often forms stronger than any other control.

What is a public opinion? As public opinion is necessarily the opinion of the public, the term 'public' must first be explained and analysed.

Public is a group so large that all the individual members may not be in direct contact with one another. The interaction between them, though not of a direct kind, gets collectively effective in the sense that their attitudes, opinions and behaviour converge to a large extent.

The members of the public to whom advertisers, editors, authors and politicians appeal through posters, books, radios, newspapers, movies, etc., are not in one place. They are scattered all over the country. Modern means of distant communication (*e.g.*, books, newspapers, movies, radio) have made the spread of ideas and attitudes possible.

Public opinion is a deeply pervasive organic force, intimately bound up with the ideological and emotional interplay of the social groupings in which gregarious individuals have come together. It articulates and formulates not only deliberative judgments of the rational elements within the collectivity, but also the evanescent common will, which somehow integrates and momentarily crystallizes the sporadic sentiments and loyalties of the masses of population.

Formation of Public Opinion: Analysis of the particular forces and processes, which are instrumental in shaping homogeneous group attitudes and pressures, calls for emphasis upon:

1. General level of socialization and the cultural media of expression prevailing in a given period;
2. The racial and national characteristics of the group;
3. The framework of political, legal and economic institution within which the process operates; and
4. Particular set of objectives towards which it may be working.

The term 'public opinion' should not be taken to imply that all members of the public hold one single opinion. Studies of public opinion have shown that on any subject at any time there are diverse opinions held by different sections of the public. Public opinion simply refers to that mass of ideas which people have expressed on a given issue.

The public opinion is not a reasoned judgment and there the word opinion is quite appropriate. It is desired that public opinion should be national but it is not always so. It is rather an attitude which people take in relation to an issue. It is usually emotionally charged, and involves beliefs, accepted principles, convictions, sentiments and firmly rooted prejudices. It is characterized by processes like personification, rationalization, etc. It is often determined by the desire to maintain the existing order of things to which the people are accustomed.

So, the formation of public opinion is obviously a complex process. The pattern of its formations is also different for different communities.

In a community, the contact between the members is direct although their minds can act in common. Hence, the public opinion in a real community should be more definite and more stable.

There are two main types of public opinion, static and dynamic. The static one (not necessarily rigid) manifests itself in the form of traditional customs, modes and usages.

The dynamic one which is predominantly rational in character is built upon the cultivated arts of persuasion and systematic publicity. It draws upon definite historical events on contemporary happenings as the material for its propaganda and agitation. This type of public opinion flourishes in the crowded streets and squares of the city, where the life of the masses unfolds under the pressure of common intercourse and exchange of opinion during the daily routine of association.

Change in Public Opinion: It is only in rural communities that the public opinion is relatively stable. But, condition of living changes as people's habits, opinions and attitudes also change. The means of ideas in a society have no longer great stability.

Modern means of indirect communication, *e.g.*, motion pictures, newspapers, radio, etc., have made it possible to stimulate the thinking of large number of men and start the process of the formation of public opinion.

6

Social Stratification

Inequalities are intrinsic as the very genetic makeup of man. Even if environmental conditions were capable of eradicating the major inequalities in human nature, the very fact remains that men must play a variety of roles. So vital or unimportant in society they would create social distinction and status differential.

Caste, broadly speaking represents a social class system in which membership is determined. In fact, there is little vertical mobility. The three upper castes formed from the Aryans were known as the twice born, because they had gone through the process of natural and physical birth and that of spiritual initiation. The four broad divisions do not by any means constitute the total complexity of the caste system.

Taya Zinkiri maintains that caste is neither class nor colour, neither occupation nor religion. He also observes on Indian Hindu Caste system a unique system of social stratification.

In fact, the ultimate sanction of the Hindu caste system is the religion and the concept of 'Karma.' It has been assumed that castes are similar to the statuses of Europe. Of course the manifold sub-castes of Indian society particularly those living in village communities are linked very closely with the economy, its division of labour and its necessary production.

Economic considerations above all, determine the class system and there is a certain correlation between the social class and the occupation pursued. Individuals in any society seek an identity with the class structure through continuous struggle for improvement of their position: Class has become associated with standards and modes of behaviour, patterns of expenditure and consumption.

Stalcup defines social class as "A level in society made up of people who consider themselves equals due to similarities in family background, level of education, occupation race and attitude toward social issues". Attempts have been made to classify occupation according to various criteria. Time has arrived when it is impossible to be precise about the criteria of class. It is less useful to talk in these terms. Groups of people may best be described by means of their role and function in the society.

SOCIAL CLASS AND EDUCATION

Emile Durkheim maintained that there were as many different kinds of education as there were social milieu in any given society. Equality of opportunity cannot be provided merely through Acts. In spite of an increasing attempt to provide conditions for equality of opportunity in education the existing social stratification inevitably presents a variety of conditions. Homogeneity and diversity are both essential ingredients in any society and any educational system.

SOCIAL MOBILITY AND EDUCATION

Social mobility is basically the movement of individuals or groups of individuals from one social position to another. Such a movement may be up or down between the classes in any social hierarchy or stratification.

Sudden appreciation of a property or power accrued to certain families, development of skill or success and achievement may lead to up word mobility. It is interesting to note a greater emphasis upon upward mobility than upon mobility downwards.

The important question now arises concerning the relationship between education and social mobility. A controversy obviously exists as to whether education acts as a sort of agent for social mobility.

THE INDIAN PERSPECTIVE

India is now in the grip of transition and the caste system is gradually losing its hold. In reality, we find a new form of stratification emerging in modern India.

It is a mixture of class system and caste system. We also find the gap between the upper and lower classes increasing day by day. The growing disparity is creating a lot of discontent and conflicts — between those who have and who have not.

In fact, the middle class contributing to the cultural heritage of India is fast withering away. The majority of people belonging to this group is facing a hard struggle for survival.

Upward mobility is only a dream for most of them. There has been a growing tendency to amass wealth in an unscrupulous way for improving the status. In spite of the dwindling caste barriers in the Indian society there is still some resistance against inter-caste marriages. Dowry system is still prevalent as a social evil.

SOCIAL STRATIFICATION AND SOCIAL MOBILITY

Social stratification is the result of social inequality. The major dimensions of stratification are power, prestige and wealth. Individuals or families in a group or society constitute a social stratum if they rank equal on a particular dimension of stratification. For example, families with income within a certain range form the same income stratum. Thus stratum is meaningful as a term only when it has a reference to the specific dimension of stratification. Some sociologists use the term social stratification in the sense of formation of fairly distinct social strata. A typical society is considered as a pyramid of ranks with the different social layers. At the bottom of the broad base lies the lower class while the narrow peak represents the upper class population. Nothing is more likely to influence the individual on the social history of a nation than the system of stratification. The nature of social stratification may vary from society to society. It, no doubt, affects the relationships and achievements of individuals and groups. Social stratification has also been called a system or institutionalized social inequality. There are obviously various forms of this stratification. For example, the caste system is based upon a rigid form of stratification, whereas in the class system the boundaries between the strata overlap as they are quite indistinct.

The bases of stratification have also to be considered for a clear understanding of the modes of interaction between the members of the society. A number of factors determine where an individual or family fits in the class-structure of a society. For example, in a caste-ridden society social status is determined almost exclusively by birth. The child of a Brahmin in India is the Brahmin for life. Similarly in every society some jobs enjoy more prestige than others. Besides wealth and income, education, prestige and privilege influence the determination of the stratum in different societies.

Social Stratification in India and the Role of Education: Two functions of education have been distinguished in respect of differentiation and selection leading to stratification. A differentiating function is held to be more pronounced in societies with a rigid system of stratification, whereas the selective function is considered to be more emphasized in open class societies. It is recognised that formal education plays a vital role in dealing with the problem of social stratification by effecting social mobility. As an agent of social change education brings more flexibility of outlook and enhances the socio-economic status of individuals even at the bottom of the rigid system of stratification. In India, today mobility is observed in both the directions vertical and horizontal as a result of education. The caste system no longer holds the same ground because of the occupational mobility. The 'Brahmins' take up various vocations without clinging to study, teaching and scholastic pursuits. Similarly the so-called 'Sudras' move up at present on the social ladder by improving their education and economic status. Thus rigid system of stratification known as the caste system has started dwindling. In fact, modern India is passing through a stage of transition in respect of values, faith and belief. The cherished values and goals are changing mainly because of impact of the western system of education and culture. The world is shrinking everyday and the specific boundaries of each culture are giving way to the new wave of ideas and ideology.

The underprivileged community so long kept in ignorance, is waking up with the dawn of emerging political consciousness. The scheduled caste, the tribal communities, the various aboriginal groups have been neglected in the past. They have been deprived of their legitimate rights of freedom of expression, education and security for ages although, they could contribute a lot to national prosperity. Similarly women in India have suffered because of the dominance of men over them. The inequality of opportunities of self-expression between people belonging to different strata and different sexes has impeded the national progress to a great extent. However, the recent education commissions have favourably considered the unprivileged classes for providing greater opportunities in the field of education and employment. This is, no doubt, a timely move in the right direction.

The stratification which exists, today, in India needs to be handled very carefully as there are certain sensitive areas demanding delicate treatment. Ignorance, poverty and prejudice which are common in the down-trodden class in India, should gradually be done away with through educational and social planning.

The traditional social structure is being influenced by major changes in the educational planning and new system of education. A gradual dissociation of occupation from caste is the result of the new emphasis on dignity of human labour. Obviously there still exists a dichotomy between manual and non-manual occupations. Although low castes are found employed more in manual occupations than in non-manual ones, the real status of a caste is not always congruent with its economic status. Of course when a caste becomes economically rich, it seeks to better its position in the caste hierarchy leading to upward mobility on the social ladder. It has been found that Western Education, particularly in India, has been one of the means of achieving upward mobility outside the framework of the caste system. Inter-caste marriage is gaining more grounds in recent times resulting in certain degrees of mobility in the social structure. Similarly the growing recognition of individual excellence irrespective of caste is contributing to social mobility as well.

Educational opportunities are still not equal as the quality of education varies according to the financial resources of the parents.

It is observed that most of the well-to-do parents tend to send their children to special schools providing western style of training and education while the municipal and local board schools are filled up by the children of lower classes and low-income groups. This, obviously, creates a form of stratification by encouraging a system of hierarchy. In other words, class-system within the framework of education is observed with all its evil consequences.

In modern India when the entire value system is in a state of flux, it is expected that significant social changes will take place as a result of the interaction between education and society. Shaping a new society with emerging values is the task of education no doubt as orienting education to the social needs is inevitable.

Social stratification which seems to be inevitable in groups is one of the most constant features of social life. Thus social stratification refers to the ranking of social positions in terms of the amount of certain desirable things associated with these positions. In most societies the most important desirable things are related to wealth, prestige and power. Thus stratification occurs in all groups. From families to entire societies within each community or a society, social classes are created by the process of ranking positions.

The importance of the social stratification in modern societies can hardly be overlooked. The problems like poverty in the midst of plenty and conflict between ethnic minority and majority groups are examples of stratification problems.

One may question, "Is social stratification inevitable? The answer is yes. As long as efficiency and control are valued in any society a form of hierarchy is bound to exist. As a variety of roles is certain, status differential would emerge. Even if inequalities are not consistent with the very genetic makeup of man, caste in India represents a social class system in which membership is determined at or by birth. The four broad divisions, *viz.*, 'Brahmin', 'Kshatriya', 'Vaisya' and 'Sudra' don't by any means constitute the total complexity of the caste system. Of course the Hindu caste system is, closed one. It is a stratification fixed for all individuals by the nature of their birth. Thus it is unique among the systems of social stratification.

While social class in our society developed, economic considerations were of prime importance in establishing new classes. Class has become associated with standards and modes of behaviour. Several classifications have been attempted by different sociologists.

Behind each from of stratification one may find some criterion or criteria which may vary from context to context. Academic excellence, intellectualism prestige and power in addition to economic status provide the basis for most of the stratifications. For example, the class structure followed in European societies is as follows:

(a) Ruling groups,
(b) Intellectual group,
(c) Service Class,
(d) Ruled Class.

It is, however, interesting to observe the following groups or strata within the Soviet society as identified by Inkles.

1. Ruling elite,
2. Superior intelligent,
3. General intelligent,
4. Working class aristocracy,
5. White colour,
6. Well-to-do peasants,
7. Average worker,
8. Average peasants,
9. Disadvantaged worker,
10. Forced labour.

7

The Concept of Social Change

The idea of social change came from the desire for betterment. There are many theories of social change. Ogburn pointed out that social changes originate in the invention by some individual of a new way of doing something or of something new to do. Hart says that social change is linear and accelerative and the direction of change is invariably toward increasing efficiency or effectiveness. But the inadequacy of this theory has also been demonstrated.

Social change comes about through the working of home process that is built into society, some inherent social process.

The a-social nature of social change has been assumed by many. Social change emerges directly out of the society.

Robert E. Park says that change comes about as an incidental consequence of the interaction of numbers or people.

Change is inevitable in society and life. There are reasons for any type of change. Social change presupposes some dissatisfaction with the existing state of affairs. There are conflicts responsible for the changes. Many factors, internal and external, contribute to any type of change. We are living in a period of rapid social change and it is often difficult to understand the reasons. While we find the external change, we also realise its implications. The principal sources of such changes are likely to be either (1) Changes in the physical environment, and (2) Changes in the social environment or any other event and influence.

1. *Changes in the Physical Environment:* Changes in the physical environment leading to social change may be classified as those which arise (1) independently of human action, (2) as a consequence of the cumulative effect of the reaction of man to his environment. It is usual that changes in the physical environment leading to social change arise from interaction of man with his environment.

   Besides changes in the physical environment, there may be changes in the social environment. A changing social environment has to face new problems for solution. Closer communication between societies inevitably stimulates diffusion. While diffusion tends to be continuous, culture traits do not spread regularly in all directions. Diffusion involves more than the simple addition of cultures which are nothing but organised systems. A trait complex which is part of one culture has to be adapted to fit into a different cultural setting.

2. *Internal Factors Effecting Change:* There are factors external as initiator of social changes, but at the same time there are factors internal having some influence on the change. Invention is a basic unit of social change and culture traits stimulate invention. The larger the culture-base, the greater is the possibility of social change.

   It is an admitted fact that culture is directly related to the amount and intensity of contact. It is, therefore, obvious that any change is bound with a number of factors. India today has faced a new problem after her independence. The previous set of ideas is becoming obsolete. The economic, political and cultural life of India is undergoing gradual changes.

   It is almost certain that man is dynamic in nature and he wants changes. The state of dissatisfaction when intensified leads to a change. This love for a change is inherent, natural and instinctive. Various types of conflict act and interact and help to develop a feeling of need for a change. In order to make any progress, this change is essential.

   Technological bias is highly responsible for the instability of a society at this age. There is nothing very stable because of the ever-changing outlook of life. Social change is sometimes a great stimulation for improvement. But too many changes abruptly brought may prove to be disastrous. There should be some amount of social security as well among the people as no culture can thrive in an ever-changing society.

3. *Education and Social Change:* Social change is a complex affair, a resultant of so many factors joining together and influencing each other in varied combinations.

Natural climate and conditions are effective in determining the social conditions. Thus with the change in the natural environment social life undergoes change. Similarly by exploiting natural, agricultural and mineral resources man has altered his environment and thereby his social life and institutions.

Migration is another instance whereby people move into new environment different from those to which they have been used. The size of population of a nation or a group has a distinct influence on its social and cultural life as well.

But the fastest social changes are brought about by scientific and technological inventions. Social change thus takes place under different pressures. For example, the press, the radio, the aeroplanes have brought the world closer by breaking the regional barriers. Through industrialisation, the typical character of rural community is fast changing. Family structure has already undergone a radical change in recent times. The joint family system is fast breaking down and new individualistic outlook is ushering in.

Factors which bring social change may be classified under the followings:

1. Environmental factors,
2. Influx of population,
3. Socio-political upheavals,
4. Technological factors,
5. Ideological factors including value system.

It is interesting to observe that the social changes take place in a mysterious way. Apart from the environmental factors, psychological factors also operate and work slowly but steadily. Education itself is a great force working behind any social change in a desired direction.

Socialisation is one of the important functions of education. The concept of democracy and world citizenship should be fostered through education. The teachers could inculcate the value of citizenship and good living through curricular and co-curricular activities. What is mostly needed is the development of leadership right from the initial stage. Teachers have to work as friend, philosopher and guide for creating in the young generation a spirit of service and co-operation, self-confidence and healthy outlook.

4. *Agencies of Education for Social Change:* Of all the agencies, family, school, church and club deserve special mention. Some of them are not very formal while a few are formal. For example, school and church are mainly formal agencies of education while the mass media of communication, like public opinion, radio, or press are basically informal agencies.

Various human organisations contribute to socialisation and social change at various stages of life.

As mentioned earlier, family is the first unit of social life having to meet the physical and emotional needs of the children. Each member of the unit has a special role and a sort of status. Social experience in the family in early childhood proves effective as a basis for the development of personality and culture. It is family which aids or subverts the larger social process through effective or ineffective social-control.

Ogburn mentions seven functions of the family in the past. These are: (1) affectional, (2) economic, (3) educational, (4) protective, (5) recreational, (6) family status, and (7) religious status. But the functions of the family never remain constant. They change from time to time according to socio-economic structure.

With the growing impact of industrialisation, the role of church or religion is also undergoing drastic change. Most of the religious ceremonies are being replaced by social functions and losing their initial force in upholding the moral and spiritual values. New forms of spiritual congregation are coming into being with our changing outlook and social order. Missions and cultural centres are trying to keep up the spirit with increasing modifications of their programmes.

Various group organisations like Y.M.C.A., Youth Welfare Associations, Red Cross, M.R.A., N.C.C. and cultural institutes have also distinct roles in contributing to socialisation.

School is itself a miniature society and has a unique position in controlling the social interactions. As cultural patterns of the society find their way into the school, so the educative forces of the school exert active influence towards social control and change. The processes of affiliation, identification, group action and interaction are among the primary means of social development. They produce an evolution of society that is formed by each new generation entering school.

8

The School and the Community

A community is an area of social living marked by some degree of social coherence, locality and community. They form the basis of community. Members of different groups share various conditions of life with varied interests. All social relationships may be found within a community.

There are primary and secondary groups in a community. There are diversified groups of people young and old, male and female with different skills and abilities living together as neighbours.

It is a face to face primary group in which many of the major functions of life are carried on co-operatively within the group itself. Primary group is a small group where people know one another with a sense of belonging. The role of the community is (a) to inculcate in its children the attitudes and values in addition to folk-ways, and (b) to set the total pattern in which the school as an institution functions.

Thus, the climate in which the school functions is set by the community.

Communities vary in the degree of their stability. Every community is bound to feel the impact of the changing elements in our culture.

The school tended to become the focus of community interest. Steps have been taken to establish and maintain school community relationships. The school-community relationship develops gradually on the basis of social interaction which is not a one way process. The school should be flexible to continually readjust its programmme in the light of the changing needs and services of the community. Similarly, the community has its responsibility to shape the curriculum and extra-curricular programmes according to changing demands of time.

In short, school community relations should be based upon a few basic principles including that of flexibility, adaptability, expansion and responsiveness to national and world-needs.

The following principles would serve as criteria for the evaluation of any programme in progress:

(a) Education is a social process in which the child shares the community consciousness. As community life is the sum total of many agencies, individuals and institutions it can be enriched by increasing the interaction and organization in which the school plays a vital role.

The community must understand, appreciate and support the varied and difficult responsibility of our schools. Similarly, education must seek to modify community patterns of behaviour through close and constant interaction. As already mentioned, the role and function of the school should be determined in the light of the needs of the specific community backgrounds of the child.

The school should develop a programme of activities and services to extend, refine and integrate human experience for all age-groups and at all levels. Changing the behaviour of individuals is not enough, education must seek to modify community patterns of behaviour through close and constant interaction with the total culture of the community.

It is obvious that the school functions in the community with a view to contributing to the total culture. There are other agencies including church and club providing opportunities for development in different directions. The school enjoys a unique privilege because of its unique position. Although the school has a dominant role, it cannot reach all the goals. It needs help and co-operation from other agencies, so that it can effectively contribute to harmony and happiness for humanity at large.

Broadly speaking, education is not limited to the classroom; it is a continuous process of interaction through the family, the play group, the church, the vast number of organizations, the community, the nation if not the world.

EDUCATION FOR NATIONAL INTEGRATION

The word integration implies harmony and synthesis. It involves a continuous process of accommodation, assimilation and adjustment.

A close understanding and mutual respect are essential for reinforcing the bond of integrations.

National integration refers to any nation within the world today. India has been known as a land of diversity. Yet there is a unity and oneness between the various states and cultures. There is a tie of amity which binds all the parts together. Unfortunately a lot of confusion has disturbed the ethnical balance in recent years. Somehow, the inner spirit of unity and harmony has lost its strength in the midst of changing values of life?

To start with, integration as a process needs elaboration. No doubt, it involves interaction between minds and entails the process of accommodation, assimilation and adjustment. Thus mutual respect and understanding are essential for strengthening integration. Psychologically the process of integration is dynamic and continuous. Of course the fluctuation occurs from time to time in the field of interaction between different people because of their differences in outlook, attitude and values.

It goes without saying that the intensity of integration depends upon the nature and direction of the forces working behind the process of interaction.

While psychological forces work behind shaping the form of interaction on the way to integration, the social and cultural forces also influence national integration. The present state of confusion over the problem of national language and education-policy has given rise to the present controversy and conflict. As a result, the regional bias is prevailing sacrificing the national interest.

It is unfortunate that national leaders today are failing to inspire people to set top priority to our national interest. States instead of the entire country are gaining prominence although states cannot flourish at the cost of nation and national welfare.

Every State like Punjab and Bihar is claiming a separate identity and self-government in contradiction with the Indian Constitution. In this way our future prospect is getting more and more gloomy. Time has come when revolution should be brought for bringing a total harmony in our national life. This can be done through education and cultural enterprises. Every educational institute should take a definite role and responsibility to instill in the minds of the young learners a desire for unity in diversity. Besides, every attempt should be made to generate national awareness through mass media of education. Even formal education can be geared to the purpose of promoting national solidarity. All the factors of education including curriculum, teacher and school environment may be employed for the purpose.

It is quite realistic to approach the problem of disintegration from a pragmatic point of view. Prejudice and ignorance are at the root of national disintegration. Lack of mutual respect and understanding lead to disharmony. Thus a constant flow of goodwill and human commission is necessary for keeping the spirit of harmony intact.

NATIONAL INTEGRATION AND EDUCATION IN INDIA

It is logical to state that the objectives of education at different levels are to be drawn from the two main sources of (i) the needs and aspirations of the people, and (ii) the needs, and aspirations of the learners. Dr. Arora[1] has re-emphasized it when he put forward the case of 'Societal needs' in the matter of curriculum planning. In a different context, Mahanta pleaded for the assessment of the needs of the people and the requirements of the nation and also for a sharp probe into their aspirations.[2]

Dr. Arora, in his attempt at identifying the 'needs' of the present-day Indian society, has drawn freely upon the recommendations of the major Indian Educational Commissions and Committees. He has referred to the ideas and thoughts of a

1. Arora, G.L. Societal Needs and School Curriculum Bulletin of the Curriculum Group, N.C.E.R.T., New Delhi-16, September 1982.
2. Mahanta, D., Indianisation of our Education-W.B.H.A., Calcutta-73, (1981), pp. 126-133.

few 'great educators' of the land, the deliberations of a number of 'Teacher-Organisations' and the findings of some educational researchers, when he has come to conclude that for 'curriculum' planning, we should consider the following four major 'needs':[1]

(a) Promotion of national integration;
(b) Acceleration of the process of modernisation;
(c) Eradication of the social inequities; and
(d) Removal of the moral injustices.

We may fruitfully recall here the suggestions made by the A.I.F.E.A. (All India Federation of Educational Associations) in their seminar on 'Education', held at Hyderabad in 1975. The A.I.F.E.A. discussed the theme 'Education', for the needs of India, today and tomorrow"[2] and suggested that the following points should be duly considered by the future curriculum-makers:

1. The long-term development plans to be launched for the growth of the nation.
2. The enterprises to be undertaken for the generation and furtherance of the new economic order.
3. The measures to be taken for the awakening and spread of 'National Consciousness'.
4. The policies to be followed for the establishment and consolidation of the new socio-political order.
5. The work programmes to be implemented for the eradication of 'ills' like poverty, illiteracy and injustice.

The UNESCO in their fourth Regional Conference (1978) on 'Education and Economic Planning in Asian Countries,' recalled the recommendations of the International Commission on "Lifelong Education" (1972) and suggested the following major areas of emphasis in the educational reform of the developing countries.[3]

I. Democratisation of educational opportunities to the optimum level and, as such, arrangements for providing educational services much more diverse in character.

---

1. Arora, G.L., Curriculum Bulletin, September 1982, *Ibid.*
2. A.I.F.E.A., Souvenir Education, Today and Tomorrow, 1975.
3. Bulletin of the UNESCO Regional Office for Education in Asia and Oceania, Number 20, June 1979, UNESCO, Bangkok, (1979) pp. iii-v.

II. Community involvement in education with necessary scope for decentralisation of educational programmes, and administration.

III. Appropriate articulation of 'Education' with 'Productive 'Work.'

While the first two areas could urge us to the strategy of 'collective movement' for a 'nation-centric' education-system, the third one would directly influence the 'structural change' and the 'curricular reform'.

Anyway, we may all agree that our education system should be better adapted to our national realities, in the form of national needs and aspirations, and that it should duly reflect the national ideals and goals that would evolve from the new Constitution of the nation. We may also agree that for the sake of national identity we should work out a common structure and devise a basic framework of the school-curriculum that would embody the broad principles and policies of our national life. The amendment to our Constitution which has placed 'Education' in the 'Concurrent List' may pave the way towards that. Necessarily, this will entail a critical review of a few of our national policies and the corresponding educational programmes.

One such policy is the policy of national identity and national integration with a truly significant implication for the education system. The divisive forces of religious fanaticism, communalism, casteism, regionalism, provincialism and linguism have occasionally been raising their ugly heads to kindle and spread the deadly fire of separatism and thereby to disturb the veritable existence of the nation. Dr. Arora has rightly listed 'National integration' as the first and foremost 'need' of the country.[1] Whatever we may think out to be the true concept of such 'identity' and 'integration', our experience of the last three decades would clearly indicate that we have to devise a new way to our 'identity' and plan a new move to our 'integration', no matter if we are to fight against heavy odds to that end. Particularly, the young generation that constitutes the

1. Arora, G.L., *Ibid.*, p. 3.

strongest force of the nation must be helped to imbibe a new 'Indian outlook' and to assimilate the new 'Indian Values' of democracy, socialism and secularism.

Ours is a multilingual country; and in a multilingual country, the language policy that is followed is normally, the most important constituent of the desired 'identity' and 'integration'. The language policy, followed so far, has resulted in the three-language formula of the education-sector, during the last thirty years. We should, however, recall that the three-language formula was only an add interim measure for the first ten years of our 'Constitutional Adventure', *i.e.*, from 1950 to 1960, and that we were required to review it in 1961. Unfortunately, however, that three-language formula has been allowed to stay unmodified, even after 1991, although it has in no way proved its worth for the intended task of national integration.

Some may be tempted to suggest that we have perhaps hung too long on a formula of dubious value and it is time for us to review the whole issue and formulate a new line of action. Moreover, it is evident that the real spirit of the three-language formula has mostly been lost sight of or deliberately neglected in many of the states, with the result that the said formula has not only proved itself un-congenial to the cause of our national identity and national integration, it has of late turned into a positive handicap. Further, the young pupils, especially those of the disadvantaged section of our population including what we call the 'first generation learners' are being increasingly overtaxed when they are compelled to learn the three components of the language. There three 'major' languages to learn as first, second and third languages are too heavy by way of supplemental language-development. The consequence is that the educational progress of the majority of our school children is seriously hampered.

Even a crude analysis of the results at the school stage will show that about 80-85 per cent of the pupils have failed in English, the so-called 'second language' in most of the States.

All these, and a few other side-effects would force us to suggest that the three-language formula should perhaps be dropped and a two-language formula be introduced in its place.[1] The two-language formula would obviously consist of the 'Regional' language as the 'first' language and the 'Official' language, as the second language. There may be provision for learning a third language, but only on an additional elective basis. Of course, the issue of the 'Federal' language of the Union should be settled immediately, in order to reduce the scope of any further disturbing situation. In an earlier article on 'National Policy on Education', it was submitted that the 'Federal' language of the Union should be so developed as to serve satisfactorily as the common language of thought and expression for the people of the country, as a whole[2]. And if so required, it should transform itself into a veritable 'Lingua Franca' for the 'States' of India. Moreover, it should also improve itself to become an adequately equipped vehicle of 'modern science and technology' that now pervades our expanding socio-cultural life. In the 1972 Annual Conference of the All India Federation of Education Associations held at Varanasi, it was pleaded that the Federal language of the Union be newly named as 'Bharatiya Bhasa' the language of Bharat (that is India). That change in the name is likely to create a favourable atmosphere of emotional acceptability.[3] Hindi, the official language of the Union, can very well be acclaimed as the national language or the language of India (that is Bharat). A vigorous 'Campaign' may immediately be made to that effect and simultaneously, we should make an all-out effort to translate the Hindi language (*i.e.*, Bharatiya Bhasa) into a real link-language of the country, through liberal incorporation of 'rich' vocabularies from other major Indian languages, just in the same way as the English language does to enrich itself continuously. In other words, our 'Bharatiya Bhasa' should also try to develop itself in such a way that it can, in the near future, claim to be compared with the richest languages of

1. Mahanta, D., Our Education in the Making, W.B.H.A., Calcutta-73. pp. 131-134.
2. Mahanta, D., National Policy on Education, Bulletin of the West Bengal Headmasters Association, Calcutta-73, March 1981, pp. 3-9.
3. Mahanta, D., Our Education in the Making, *Ibid.*, p. 133.

the world. Such a conception of our 'Federal language' would easily reinforce the new spirit of the democratic, socialistic and secular Republic of Bharat. If the choice of Hindi as the official language of the Union was dictated earlier by the decision about 'Bharatiya Bhasa, the federal language of the country should now be taken to consolidate the sense of 'Bharatiyata' (Indianhood) and thus to give a new tone to the intended goal of an integrated, unified nationality and to boost up the 'morale' of the people to that end.[1]

Of course, change in the language-policy is not the end all of an 'alternative solution' to the pressing problem of national integration as there are other vital issues as well.

1. Mahanta, D., National Policy on Education, Bulletin of W.B. Headmasters Association, Calcutta-73, March 1981, pp. 3-9.

9

The Present Scene in Indian Society

Sociologically speaking India is in the grip of transition. It seems that everything is at the cross-road at this crucial hour when experiments are being made in different fields. In fact, the old tradition is crumbling down while some of the new values are emerging. It is also interesting that some old fashions and styles are taking new forms and dimensions, but basically they are not changing.

Historically, we have come to the end of British Raj system when the left out values have almost disappeared. The needs and interests are changing but still there is a fad for some British cults and culture. Speaking good English, wearing good suits are still regarded as signs of aristocracy. It is quite usual to have and interplay between the various values and cults in the shrinking world today.

It would be helpful if we take up the following perspectives for discussion with a view to doing justice to this topic.

(a) Family structure in transition;

(b) The community life of today;

(c) Individualism and group-life;

(d) Our changing education;

(e) The present mass media for dissemination of culture as contrasted to that of the past;

(f) The present trends in Indian economy and its impact on our day-to-day life; and
(g) Our changing values and lifestyle.

(a) Family Structure in Transition

As mentioned earlier, our family is a very important unit of our society. For obvious reasons it is the breeding ground of values, culture and education. A good personality develops in a good family and so a good education. It is thus important to discuss the role of family in the present social context of India.

As family is not merely a conglomeration of different numbers. It is an effective environment, a common forum and a shelter for sharing joys and sorrows, ideas and sentiments. India has built up a very effective family unit where it absorbs both young and old, present and past generations. It is a joint family system which has been easily introduced to cope with the challenges of Indian economy and values. There are certain deep-rooted values of tradition in Indian culture, which not only includes utilitarian modalities of life but also few permanent modes based on faith, creed and experiences. For example, respect for the old people, compassion for the poor and hospitality are all projections of Indian values. It is a fact that most of them belong to some attitude towards life which has been accepted after long practice.

As a result of the drifting of values our family structure is changing fast. The unit is becoming smaller where only husband and wife with their children prefer to live together. Unlike in the past there is not much place for other relatives and even the old parents within the family at the moment. This kind of situation has been the outcome of the changing attitude and values in addition to other factors economic and social. There is a shrinking self-centered outlook which we find today influencing our social interaction. For some reasons the heart to heart dialogue between the old and the new members of the family is becoming difficult. Very often we call this 'generation gap'. In fact, the affinity and cohesion among the family members are gradually eroding and often we find conflicts and confrontations in the field of interaction between father and son, brother and other family members. In the community life we find the same picture. There is not hardly any respect and love, nor is there any tolerance and understanding at any level in the society at large.

It is thus extremely disappointing to find disharmony and disintegration within the family and community, states and the nation. One may wonder around this picture of the present society so dismal and frustrating. The answer is not that easy to be put in a few words. It seems that the entire world is at unrest and on the way to a drastic change. It looks that man today is becoming desperate to find a new way of life without knowing what he wants. This terrible passion just for a change in his values and lifestyle is bursting out in various forms with various expressions. It appears that he has never become so unhappy as he is today. Maybe, he is unhappy with himself, with his own performance. When he looks back it is not difficult for him to realise the mistakes he has committed in ignoring the human values and putting priorities to the superficial and materialistic pursuits. Truly speaking he is in a trap at this time of confusion and crisis. Neither he can turn back as it is too far from the traditional goal, nor is it easy for him to have a smooth journey towards what he wants. This is a sort of confusion in his conduct and attitude projected in every walk of life.

(b) The Community of Life Today

An analytic study of the community life and events today reveals some significant behaviour pattern of the community people today.

The members of the family and community are seeking some satisfaction from outside and are on the lookout for external stimulation. Somehow, they are not getting satisfaction within the family as they used to do in previous days. The economic status of a family is held in esteem and the culture and tradition are secondary. At the time of matrimonial connection the cultural and social status was once regarded very important. But now-a-days family status is judged more by the wealth and possessions the family has got. The values attached to the quality of a marriage were also different. The daughter looked for the beauty of the bridegroom; the mother looks for the wealth, the father for the status and the rest for the sweetmeats. Unfortunately, our present community could not escape the irrational trend of accepting dowry in some form or other. The situation has not changed much as it tells upon the nerve of the daughter's father to meet the expectation of the bridegroom. This is one of the maladies of our society which theoretically denounces the dowry system. There are so many other examples of social injustice and disharmony and inequality. Marriage at an early age of minority groups, 'sati-daha' system in certain communities, caste barriers, religious prejudices are few of the numerous examples of our social disequilibrium.

(c) Individualism and Group-life

No doubt, individuals form the society and community, yet, the social norms and the community constraints are hard to ignore. For a healthy society, the conformity to social roles is essential. Individuals have obligations to comply with the dictations of social ethics and jurisprudence, no matter what their preference is. Obviously, there are instances of various conflicts, arising out of strong individualities and attitude of community members. They tend to defy the social norms and stand out ignoring their obligations to the community. As a result, anti-social groups are forming almost within each community today. There is not much control to regulate their conduct and set them in order. The present age of transition is an age of experimentation when the chaos and confusion are allowed to prevail.

Recently, people are becoming more conscious of their individual needs and comforts without much regard for the group and community in which they live. Somehow, they prefer individualism to altruism. Maybe, our present culture and education encourage this self-centered outlook and prompt the people to seek personal gratification. Priorities have been set without much reason, to individualistic goals. Examples of narrow outlook and self-gratification are everywhere.

While this tendency is prevalent in the modern society we feel handicapped and isolated for want of co-operation and unified strength. When there was a joint family system every member used to feel self-confident to combat any external threat or aggression, in spite of their limited economic resources. It is hard denying the fact that money is not the only strength, it is man-power which is also very important. In a joint family one could feel secure in the group-life they used to live, where brothers, parents and even cousins used to have a common life under the same roof. Besides, there was a fellow feeling among the neighbours and community members, particularly in the villages. They used to spend their days and hours together with mutual feeling of trust, tolerance and co-operation. Each village was a cultural unit, a centre of community activities and group interaction.

Individuals and groups are supplementary and there is a need for compromise for a healthy adjustment to one another. It is imperative that any compromise needs sacrifice and tolerance which we are lacking today. Of course there is a tendency to form different groups like clubs and associations in towns and villages today. People tend to share their ideas and experience through these associations. In addition, there are big organisations like Lions Club, Rotary Club, almost in every big town. Both adults and youngsters participate in activities organised by the clubs and interact quite freely in various ways. In villages as well, the students organise games and sports, through their clubs. There are different 'samitis' (committees), like 'Puja Samiti' for observing the various religious festivals. Thus, we find that the group-life of individuals is enriched through such organisations and their activities. Cultural programmes including drama, music, recitation are also arranged by the literary clubs or libraries in towns and villages. The number of such organisations is gradually increasing today with a view to sharing the emotions and sentiments around ideals and beliefs of people. The individuality is, therefore, retained and projected through suitable channels and forms, although a group-life demands adjustments and sacrifices.

As mentioned earlier, we find our villages changing their character and their tendency towards urbanisation. The number of educated people is every village is increasing and superstitions and prejudices are giving way. Besides there is a growing awareness of party politics in every village and in many cases the minor conflicts among the villagers are handled by the parties themselves and not by the courts of law. Unfortunately, our villages are still neglected and there is not much improvement in transportation. This is a definite hindrance to mobility of the rural population.

(d) Our Changing Education

Education is the backbone of a nation and the national progress takes place through education. It is observed that since independence, India has made several attempts to bring changes in educational system as well as policy. Various commissions have been set up by the government with a view to reviewing the educational system, but with no tangible success. Experiments are going on emphasising the curricula or the examination system. Unfortunately, the human factors are yet to be given prominence for real improvement of our educational system. The teacher-pupil relationship, the ideology of the teachers, the team spirit within the school, the teacher-parent liaison and the school community interaction have yet to improve a lot for building up an effective system of education. The pupils have been treated like guinea pigs in the experimental set up. The load of syllabus is increasing by leaps and bounds, ignoring the limited capacity of the young learners. Certain bias is projected in the name of new experiments of education. Moreover, there have been attempts to exploit the sentiments of the people around certain basic issues like vocational education and employment opportunities through education. If there is a mix-up between the two, it is doubtful if we could reach a real satisfactory end. It is, of course, the responsibility of education to help the learners to be self-sufficient in life but we cannot put the cart before the horse. We should never forget that education has to look after the personality development first and then the vocational adjustment. There should be certain basic education which is imperative for building up healthy citizens in all respect. Very recently, we hear of Navodaya School where we find some new ideas injected through education. It may be a good idea to relate education to life theoretically but there should be a continuity of the educational programme to lead to vocational ends. Moreover, one should not forget that India is a land of democracy where we have got to ensure equality of opportunity as a principle. In the Navodaya system, however, we find certain tendencies towards encouraging class system. In other words, those who would get opportunities in the Navodaya system would be eventually privileged to rule over the rest.

(e) The Present Mass Media for Dissemination of Culture as Contrasted to That in the Past

In all ages various media of expression have been used. Even the scripts on the marble or on the barks of the trees have served the purpose in the past. Gradually, writing has been introduced to indicate a giant leap in the history of civilisation. Since then, books and journals have been able to serve as an effective mass medium of education. But the books were beyond the reach of the illiterate people. It was, therefore, felt that there is a need for mass media through which the people in general could gather knowledge and information. Pictures, models and music used to serve the purpose. There is obviously an appeal of sound of music as well as projected picture. The audio-visual stimulations generate interests to a great extent. This is why audio-visual aids are indispensable in the classroom today. Films and cassettes are used more than ever for making lessons interesting for creating interest in a lesson. Unfortunately, many schools of rural India are not even equipped with good blackboards, charts, maps and globes, not to speak of films and cassettes. Yet, we can hardly deny the effectiveness of these media particularly at the age of knowledge explosion. When competition is ever on its increase, a young learner is expected to cope with that challenge without much choice. At home and in school we have now a scope for availing of the radio, television and videos in the affluent societies. But there is a disparity between the two worlds, namely, the rich and the poor, the privileged and the deprived. Democracy in education has got to do something to bring some parity and uniformity. Beyond the Atlantic we find a tremendous conquest of computer science in every field of life, including commerce and education. Life without computer is incomplete in the countries like U.S.A. It is no wonder that computer has been much in use even in the classrooms of the United States. It is a sophisticated aid no doubt but it is very unique and helpful in learning.

(f) The Present Trend in Indian Economy and its Impact on Our day-to-day Life

Indian economy has taken its turn from its conservative to aggressive direction. The old concept of economics has completely changed as it no longer believes in self-sufficiency on individual basis. The world today believes in interdependence and mutual exchanges of trade and commerce. For facilitating the exchange of trade and business export and import rules have drastically changed and there have been many relaxations in foreign trade and commerce. The Commonwealth countries have established a trade organisation for exchange of expertise. In this perspective we can easily conclude by saying that free flow of money and ideas is the main objective of the international trade today.

Indian economics has also been influenced by the modern concept of international trade. The World Bank has been set up for granting loan and advance for trade expansion in different countries. India has improved her economic position by expanding her export market and restricting the scope for import, by means of self-sufficiency in those areas. For example, she has brought green revolution by improving her farming operations and the programme of production of small tools, gadgets and equipments. Even India is earning a lot from the foreign tourists as it has been trying to set up strategies as on industry.

So far as our village economics is concerned, we find some changes as well. There has been a steady flow of capital from outside since the cottage industries including the handlooms, special handicrafts, and clay modelling have created interest and found some market, even in foreign countries.

With the introduction of small industries in towns and suburbs, we find some mobility among the villagers, particularly the women-folk. The cost of labour has gone up considerably and sometimes it is hard to get their services when we need them. With this changing economy we find our increasing wants in our day-to-day life. Our needs are multiplied with the growing complexity of our life.

(g) Our Changing Values and Lifestyles

Modern amenities have increased and people are no longer satisfied with their plain living and high thinking. The cost of living is much higher, with the change of our lifestyle. People have started side business for supplementing their income.

SCHOOL AND COMMUNITY

The development of school idea has been continuous since long. During ancient time the 'Gurugriha' was the most effective school and the 'guru' was the friend philosopher and guide of the young learners. He was concerned with the total development of the young disciple who was sent to him in good faith by the community. The 'guru' enjoyed the highest esteem as he had no mercenary motive. The disciple was a full-time student under the total care and guidance of the 'guru'. He was asked to do various things, *viz.*, planting, gardening, tending cows, tilling soil, cutting of woods, etc. Besides every disciple used to gain knowledge and wisdom sitting under his feet. So unlike the modern schools, 'Gurugriha' was meant for creating personalities and creative people, leaders and academicians. With the growing demand of mass education formal schooling was introduced. There were 'chatuspathis' set up by Sanskrit scholars and 'pathshalas' by village teachers before the sophisticated schooling started. No matter what form of schooling emerged from time to time, the need for community participation was felt more and for a meaningful education. After all, the aim of education was mainly to socialise the individual if not to humanize him. Both the individual and social aspirations were expected to merge at a point for making individual life and living geared to social needs and expectations. The pupils were expected not only to learn various subjects and subject-matter but also to grow as a social being. With a view to meeting these objectives social studies and social work have been incorporated in the syllabus at different levels of education. Credits have been given to extra-curricular activities and socio-cultural participation within the school. N.S.S. programmes, boys scout participation and such other adjunct programmes for socializing individuals have been included in the total framework of education. Nevertheless, education has been considered as a tool or medium for helping individuals to grow in every direction.

We live in a society, in a community and in a family, we cross our individual boundaries and extend ourselves in the context of the community and the society. We learn to behave to comply with the social norms, to fulfill the ambition of becoming a healthy citizen of the world. So the school today is regarded as a miniature society where there are lots of interaction, interests and events. The teachers including the head teacher are just like the guardians of the school community responsible for regulating the conduct of the growing pupils. There are also certain goals set up in the individual schools and attempts are made to reach these goals in a number of ways. The pupils grow through social and group interactions. It takes various forms like co-operation, competition and conflicts, within the classroom, in the sports ground and even outside campus. They interact and learn from one another, sharing experiences through participation in group-life in games, sports, dramatic activities and cultural functions. School thus becomes a replica of a community within its limited infrastructure. The different types of members, who come in contact with the school authorities and management, teachers and pupils are guardians, public and visitors from different walks of life. The school administration should wisely give a wide scope for such exchanges of visit, views and experiences. A good school is one which tries to maximize this interaction between people at all levels from different corners of the community. It should organise regular socio-cultural functions, ceremonies and celebrations, inviting community members to actively participate, in every way. There should be a scope for community participation in school life by means of active involvement of the members in school programmes. Cultural functions, exhibitions, sports, birthday celebration, new year's days are the occasions for encouraging the social interaction in the school life.

Teaching is a part of teacher's function but not his entire role. He has the responsibility to create different learning situations to encourage the pupils to participate in various forms of interaction. Instead of lecturing, the teacher could encourage group discussions for free flow of ideas between one group and the other. In this way, the classroom situation should be more stimulating. The pupils should come up with new ideas and feel free to express themselves even in a non-traditional manner. Thus the classroom should represent a community where members are allowed to interact freely and share experiences before taking a decision or reaching a goal. Thus a community life should be projected within the classroom and school life for making the school community relation really conducive to education.

Regarding evaluation and examination we find that there is still a traditional approach which needs to be changed for improving the system. Instead of focussing upon the individual assessment, attempt is being made to encourage group assessment by setting various groups and taking the total performance of each group into consideration.

This approach will help the individual members of the class to build up a team spirit and a co-operative attitude. They will learn and live together. The idea of bringing a co-operative spirit in place of individual self-centered outlook is the most befitting one during this age of transition. As observed by a professor of Sociology, there is one aspect of the development of the societies which disturbs observers of history that is the persistence of evil. It is interesting to observe that economic crisis and famine have been faithful companions of human race. Evil is a historical necessity and the creation of a social order without evil has so far proved impossible. It goes without saying that the individuality and society are often at conflict and that leads to some changes in social order. Individuality is also free of all things which arise in the sphere of what is common and similar. Within the providence of individuality man transcends what is common and similar. He is, therefore, alone. Every group creates a system of mores, customs and opinions, penalties and rewards which are also set as behaviour control.

From the above observations one can conclude that the individuals merge into groups as individuality fuses the society.

School provides the platform for such a fusion through planned programmes of curricular and co-curricular activities.

Today a school can hardly exist without a close and effective interaction with the community. Each contributes to the total growth of the individuals living in social context. It is the task of the school and community to come closer for more effective operation in the interest of the society at large. In fact, the well-being of a society depends upon a happy and harmonious relationship between the school and the community. It is thus very clear that home has a major role in strengthening the tie and affinity between the school and community. The parents and the teachers have to take positive roles for making this dream a reality. School is thus a community centre, a centre which echoes the spirit and aspiration of the greater society. The pupils are our future hope and it is through their functions and co-operative enterprise a community life will be enriched.

10

An Analysis of Some of the Problems in India in Educational Perspectives

"The world is today passing through one of the greatest crises in its history. Shaken to its foundation by the Great War. it has not yet been able to pick up the thread of normal progress. The political, social and economic doctrines on which the progress of the nineteenth century appeared to be founded have given way in some countries to complete uncertainty as to the next step....," says I. L. Kandel in his "Studies in Comparative Education".

It is, therefore, wise to take into account socio-economic structure of the present society of India with implications.

Again the socio-economic problems rest on several factors of which population with its manifold aspects deserves special attention. This factor of population has particular reference to the sex ratio, the influx of population due to heavy immigration in India, the typical problems due to marriage, infant mortality and want of suitable occupations.

On the other hand, the problems which are more economic in nature have a special reference to mal-distribution of wealth owing to the several factors, *viz.*, wrong approach to the policy of production, procurement, consumption and control. Particular reference is also necessary to the factors like non-equitable division of labour, concentration of wealth in the hands of the few, problem of unemployment and wastage of energy of the young-folk due to want of proper guidance, etc.

Next come a number of problems which are pivotal and which have got a close connection with the defects of the social structure of the day. These may be described as social disintegration and social stratification with their ramifications such as the caste system, racial prejudices, narrow provincialism, blind faith in social customs and traditions.

Thus, the socio-economic problems are mostly due to several inherent defects in the present social structure. Besides these, another factor appears to play a predominant part in the society. That is the psychological mal-adjustment which is deepening the crisis all the more and extending the dimension of the problems. Particular reference should, therefore, be made to the manifold aspects of these crucial problems, such as lack of mutual trust and emotional stability. Russell believes in the propaganda and the possibility of solution of problems through education. Thus he says, "One of the most important parts of education, and one of the most neglected, is that which teaches how to reach true conclusions on insufficient data."

Problem of Population

It is a fact that the proportion of the population of India living on agriculture is very large and it has been steadily on the increase. It will be seen that the percentage of real agricultural class is on its decrease. Most people who have got no other alternative but to take up agriculture as vocation of life. They are compelled to be directly or indirectly dependent on land or cultivation. As a result, the landless cultivators, increasing at a rapid rate are inviting poverty and financial deadlock.

The Royal Commission on Agriculture has pointed the same melancholy tale which is still true. "The overcrowding of the people on the land, the lack of alternative means of securing a living, the difficulty of finding any avenue of escape and the early age with which a man is burdened with dependents, force the cultivators to grow food wherever they can and on whatever terms are available."

This is the observation on the agricultural position of the whole of India, but so far as West Bengal is concerned the situation is more precarious. The influx of population in West

Bengal due to heavy immigration after the partition, as well as the irreparable loss of the most suitable lands for cultivation because of the same reason has made the food situation more complex and alarming. When Bengal had an area of 77,442 sq. miles with fertile soil mostly in East Bengal districts, it was even then very difficult for the province to carry a burden of few crores of population.

It is, therefore, not difficult to imagine the present position of West Bengal when almost 60 per cent of her the best productive land has been included in Bangladesh, whereas the number of displaced persons is on its increase. Dr. Radha Kamal Mukherji observes the position of Bengal before partition with reference to cultivable land and says that the area cultivated by a cultivator comes to 47 acres as compared to 0.63 in U.P. and 0.74 in Madras. Dr. R.K. Das in his "Industrial Efficiency of India" has shown that the problem of population has become more acute not only due to rapid increase of population but largely because of wastage of our resources. It is a fact that the percentage of total land cultivated is very small in comparison with the area which West Bengal contains. This is partly because of the gradual deterioration of soil particularly in West Bengal due to the stagnant condition of the rivers after the British invasion of this land.

According to the observation made by Dr. Radha Kamal Mukherji, "Nearly half of cultivable land in the Districts of Burdwan and Hooghly have been almost surrendered during last 30 years owing to the deterioration of river system due to embankments and Railway Bridges." Besides these, there are other States as well. These factors may be described as follows:

1. The over pressure of the population on agriculture, through the blocking of other economic channels.
2. The effects of land-monopoly and of the burdens of the peasantry.
3. Poor technique due to ignorance and prejudice of the cultivator class.
4. The sub-division and fragmentation of holdings, the individualistic petty farming due to the socio-political influence.

5. Negligence of soil due to want of proper manuring, irrigation system and supervision in the light of modern science.

This neglect is not only from the cultivators but form the state also. This has been observed by many who have ascribed the alarming features of this deterioration of soil partly due to negligence in various forms. Very recently, there has been some change in the Government policy for improvement.

R. Palme Dutta in his "India To day", observes the following typical features and problems so far as agriculture is concerned. He says, "The agricultural population of India still works on very meager resources which, if we consider the well-being of the peasant themselves, are very poorly distributed. He also considers malaria, malnutrition and such other diseases as another cause of this deterioration in agriculture. It is worthwhile to quote a report of the Bengal Irrigation Department Committee in 1930. This report throws some light on the agricultural position of the states, "Central Bengal is at present a decadent tract: it is malarias, the population is steadily decreasing, and the land is going out of cultivation. It may, of course, be the case that the deterioration has already preceded so far that it cannot now be checked, and that the tract in question is doomed to revert gradually into swamp and jungle." But this is not all. The overcrowded cultivators within this limited cultivated area, the social condition, the paralysing burdens placed on them their extreme poverty and primitive technique mean that while the demands on the land are heavier, the level of production is lower than in any country. Many questions arise in connection with labour and capital as regards the crisis in agriculture of India. J.H. Hutton, C.I.E, has raised a very significant point in connection with the improvement of agriculture which also may be applied in connection with the study of agriculture position of Bengal.

The total mechanisation of agriculture, he points out, will reduce the need for labour and will do little for solving labour problems though there is no scope for doubt about its suitability in the present crisis. It is, therefore, really controversial whether mechanisation will help to solve all the economic problems, and whether this will be rendered feasible under the present conditions of India.

In this connection Tarlok Singh in his "Poverty and Social Change" has made a very valuable discussion on the practical side of the problem. He says, "Any system of co-operation in agriculture has, therefore, to answer two basic questions: First, what are we to do with ownership in land? Second, how is the work to be allotted and evaluated? He further observes that the present owners and hereditary tenants form the backbone of India's agriculture. They are the heart and the substance of the civilization and of the social values which the village community represents today. In re-organising our rural economy, we must have the peasants with us and not against us. But it is equally essential in the ultimate interest of the peasants themselves that ownership should be dissociated from control over the use of separate bits of land within the village. It is, therefore, suggested by him to take up unit of the village as a whole for cultivation and to distribute the return on the basis of the ownership of the capital and the land which they have contributed to the village farm. Thus joint village management is perhaps the most concrete and immediately practical form which can replace the traditional system of individual ownership. This will solve not only the economic problem but also help to bring about social integration and harmony. When the village will begin to function effectively as an economic unit in agriculture and in relation to industry, the present division into groups will tend to be modified and all sections of the community including the depressed classes may hope to achieve equal opportunity and equal freedom.

Though different problems might crop up for the time being on the way to transforming the present economy by rapid change, they may still be tackled and controlled by suitable organisations and managements. But major group of problems which arises from the rationalisation of agriculture is really complicated. Even at the present moment "there is a great deal of underemployment or disguised unemployment in agriculture." Tarlok Singh also observes that "the increase in population deepened the poverty of rural artisans, field labourers and village servants and not many among them have full and regular employment in their own occupation." The question naturally arises as to how surplus thrown up as a result of the rationalisation of agriculture will be absorbed and how their financial position can be improved. This requires the establishment of a social instrument which will explore and create avenues of employment by a simultaneous development of industry throughout the land. Instead of large-scale industrialisation, if small industry can be grown in rural areas on the basis of local products in order to meet the local demands, the problem of urbanisation and unemployment can, it is hoped, be solved to a great extent. In other words, jointly managed villages can act as sub-producers working in liaison with organised industry. For this the village artisans, the skilled labourers should be better organised, equipped and trained and the great deal of processing of local products can be done in the villages by the villagers themselves.

It is thus seen that considerable integration between rural and industrial economy must be ensured and a social control should come up to facilitate this integration. As discussed before, education can help a lot to improve the social and economic position of people particularly the cultivator class, handicapped by all means. It is, therefore, suggested that effective plannings of education should be put into practice for effective solution.

The Royal Commission on Agriculture in India suggests various ways and methods of improving agriculture, the most important of which is the opening of agricultural research centres in different areas whose function will be not only to discover the causes of deterioration but to carry experiments on manual problems, on fertilisation of soil, on hybridisation and acclimatisation.

In the circumstances, it is imperative that the lot of problems around soil, irrigation, the finance of agriculture such as poultry, fishery, etc., should attract the notice of the educational engineers as well. Education should take up certain responsibilities in improving the socio-economic position of people involved and as such definite well-planned methods and programmes should be adopted while constructing the curriculum and system of training.

The defects of the educational system so long in vogue, have been realised by many and the objectives of education should be more embracing and suitable to meet the socio-economic needs of people than in the past. But all these pious wishes have not so far been able to bring about any thorough reform in this field. Needs of rural population have rather been neglected and the community needs ignored in the school curriculum and educational programme.

Special schools whether part-time or full-time are also to be started for training up the actual cultivators. Classes should be held in the evening or other suitable time so as to allow them to go on as usual with their daily routine of work. Practical classes, in actual field should be held for training them to use up-to-date means of cultivation, fertilisation of soil and production. Vacations of these schools should ordinarily cover the period of monsoons when they are required to toil in fields from morning till night. Besides practical education to the agricultural population, should be imparted for imparting social education which will help them to be socially conscious, medically fit and economically more equipped. These social and civic educations are essential for enlightening them in every sphere of life.

In short, the education for the rural population mostly consisting of cultivator and artisans classes should cope with the various problems in respective fields including economic development, education and public health. The essence of effective cultivation consists in combining four separate factors, *viz.*, area, capital, technique and organisation, but each of the factors is dependent on education and training for the utilisation of these by people. It is, therefore, the task of education to reorganise peasant villages so that the chief factors, capital and organisation can fully play their parts. Many suggest co-operative farming as one of the solutions to the problem of fragmentation of holdings by individual owners. Co-operative farming is one of the means to solution for rationalisation of agriculture, but it can hardly be denied that under the present system and social condition there are many difficulties and barriers on the way to this formidable task.

The peasants who form the backbone of the society, are not unfortunately conscious of their own good and national welfare, and there is every chance that they will not easily submit to State control which is primarily required for thorough mechanisation. It is the task of education to remove from their minds all prejudices and narrowness of outlook as well as to foster in them a healthy co-operative spirit. Really speaking, due to ignorance and want of sufficient care, vast areas suitable for gardening or poultry remain neglected. As a result, malaria spreads. The same may be said about the low lands which ordinarily yield one crop annually and then remain mostly un-cultivated throughout the rest of the year. But modern methods have helped the cultivators in getting many returns of crop out of the same soil in a year. The successive returns of crop throughout the year due to the scientific treatment of the soil many improve the food position considerably.

Various recreational centres are essential for the successful operation of the scheme as these will help not only to break the monotony of their life by catering joy and amusements but also to spread literacy and develop good sense among them. Films, television, radio and such other educational media should be utilised to supplement the programme of social and vocational education for the peasants. Social consciousness and co-operative spirit, proper encouragement and inspiration should also be fostered. In this connection, it is perhaps wise to impress on them the necessity of birth control and neat decent living. Periodic exhibitions, and other media will be of great help in creating a healthy climate for mutual understanding, exchange of ideas and experience.

Education for leisure is one of the crying needs of the hour not only among the peasants but also among the educated mass. In the present economic crisis, any one finds it extremely difficult to subsist on a particular occupation. A subsidiary income may be derived by utilising the idle hours in gardening, pottery, weaving, carpentry and such other sundry works. These are profitable and at the same time recreational is a necessity.

Similar measures are to be adopted so far as other vocations such as pottery, woodwork and such other pursuits are concerned. Schools for theoretical and practical training should also be started so as to suit the actual needs and demands of the locality and also to utilise the natural resources of the locality to the greatest possible extent. Thus, in the area suitable for paddy growing, agricultural schools should be supplemented with rice-mills, similarly the areas suitable for cotton and jute production require the development of small-scale textile and jute industries. The same thing may be said of the area where mustard or linseeds are sufficiently grown. Not only this, the soiled and the mineral resources should attract the attention of the Planning Department so that suitable industry can utilise these resources for increasing the national wealth. People or state should start a network of small-scale industries in rural area of India, as feeder industries, mostly to meet the local demands and solve local unemployment problems. The production of raw materials and the further utilisation of these products through industry should go hand in hand for their most successful operation. This co-ordination will help, it is hoped, the real solution of varied problems of over population to a great extent.

Moreover, education of many-sided character and the demonstration of an effective educational programme are essential for meeting the economic distress of the common mass of people. Scheme of agricultural and industrial education must both precede and follow the scientific development of India's agriculture and industries. Until such widely planned industrial and agricultural education becomes possible, the necessity of vocational bias in general education cannot be questioned on the following grounds, (i) it trains the practical intelligence of the pupils, and (ii) it further fits them to divert their capacity for earning a livelihood into diversified channels.

It is really controversial whether general education should be left aside and industrial education should only be encouraged. In the circumstances, it is wise to introduce a co-ordinated system of general, agricultural and industrial education so that no single aspect of life should be totally ignored. It is beyond any doubt that the primary task of education today is to prepare the vast illiterate mass of population, to find out avenues of employment. For the educated middle class plan to foster a national and social consciousness may be taken up.

If we try to visualise the position of different classes of population, it will be evident that much harm is due to lack of proper soul education amongst them. Infant mortality, early marriage, dowry system, social disintegration, over birth of children and premature death of majority of population are partly due to human follies and want of adequate education and planning. It will, therefore, be the function of education to remove all the evils by infusing knowledge and developing proper attitude and skills as well as to place higher ideals and noble missions before them.

So far we have discussed mostly about the various problems of rural community particularly about agricultural population, and suggestions have also been made for their best possible solution. It will, therefore, be proper to discuss the other factors of population problem. Beveridge in his book "Full Employment in a Free Society (1945)" observes, "Adequate and healthy housing presents the largest single objective for desirable outlay after the war and affords the largest scope for raising the standard of life, health and happiness." This urbanising tendency has not only affected the health and happiness of people of the city but also the education and culture to a great extent. City life has become most unsuitable for the real learners and particularly the beginners owing to the fact that the poise and tranquillity, the calmness and concentration which are essential for good education are badly lacking in cities. Besides the various corruptions which are so common in the cities and towns attract the attention of the tender aged pupils and exercise ominous influence on their life. The plenty of sun-shine and air, the restful life, the natural beauty which are in abundance in village life are beyond expectation in town life.

Moreover, the types of education which they receive in schools are quite inadequate for the development of their mind and body. Most of the town-schools are situated in busy centres of the city, housed in wretched buildings without any extra space for the movement of the students. More or less, with meager equipments these institutions run on a commercial line and very little care is taken by the school authorities to pay individual attention. Many schools can hardly provide suitable accommodation for the students, who sometimes huddle together in dark unventilated rooms and begin to count the unpleasant hours of the school. It is really unfortunate that the number of such schools in the cities is large where neither their body nor minds are stimulated. It may be mentioned here that members of the teaching staff appointed in the institutions are not enough in proportion to roll strength. They are uninspired and can hardly impress anything good on the minds of the student. Nor can they inspire and give proper guidance.

On the other hand, the villages have been depopulated as a result of which the village schools cannot get sufficient number of students for running the establishment, nor can they arrange better equipments for teaching for a very thin population due to obvious sociological reasons. The contrast of pictures in town and rural areas is thus very prominent. In towns, the student population cannot properly be accommodated, whereas in village schools there is a very poor roll-strength some time inadequate for running an institution. The question arises, therefore, as to what should be the real solution. The problem of urbanisation, though complicated, may to a certain extent, be solved by redistribution of population over the country. The villages should again be made centres of learning and the seats of higher education may be established in suitable rural areas.

The next fundamental problem which is of no less significance in the field of education is of sex-ratio in a growing population. Though a lot of confusion prevails at present regarding the problems of population and sex-ratio still many believe that in the absence of a gradual increase of population of both the male and female in equal proportion, many social evils are bound to come up. It is really unfortunate on the part of India, that parents with numerous offspring's were once the objects of venerations. The proud mother is now forced to hang her head down in shame. This is all the more when a mother gives birth to a female child particularly in the middle class family. She thinks it to be a guilt on her part to give birth to a female child and takes her to be a family burden from the very day she first sees the light. But one of the striking phenomena which are of considerable concerns to a sociologist is that even in the 1951 census there has been a definite although a small decline in the number of females per thousand males in almost every district of West Bengal except Hooghly and Calcutta. This has given rise to fresh problems in the society. This gradual decline of female population in Bengal entails a number of factors of which marriage is of great significance. On a critical analysis, it will be seen that marriage is not encouraged by the present circumstances, though it is a natural condition for men and women. As a result of the economic stringency, the marriageable age is being gradually shifted and the health of the young population is gradually deteriorating. Besides, there are several other social evils which are faced today. The consequences of these are not far to seek. The children born are mostly constitutionally weak, intellectually, over-burdened, and in particular cases handicapped due to various reasons. Moreover, the female population married at a very late stage are often victimised by premature death during the time of delivery resulting in a complete mal-adjustment in the domestic environment. On the other hand, if we look at the male population of this category, it will be noticed that they often die prematurely leaving, their dependents completely helpless and deserted. As a result, the young children lose every hope of life, and are deprived of educational opportunities and often take up undesirable courses of life. Of course, the present economic situation is mainly responsible for these evils, but at the same time it cannot also be totally denied that the present education has changed the outlook of people, who hesitate in taking the responsibility of family before they can reach their ideal standard of living. But unfortunately in most cases they are engaged in wild goose chase and when they exhaust their energy and youth, they reluctantly enter into family life. Education has thus proved a hindrance in many cases to timely marriage by creating high ambition, in their minds.

So far as sex-ratio is concerned biological factors can be traced at the root of any disproportion between male and female population. This particular phenomenon of sex-ratio has a considerable bearing on society and education. If the number of male members is greater, then women become rare and various corruptions reveal; on the other hand, if the number of male members is less, marriage problem becomes acute on the part of the bride's party and the above problem of industrial units is faced by the country due to shortage of young men. Male members persist in demanding wealth and dowry from the party of the bride.

Fortunately or unfortunately, West Bengal has a higher ratio of males leading to many far-reaching consequences in society and education. Many biologists are of opinion that children of young healthy parents are the best physically endowed and, therefore, the most desirable from the racial point of view.

Some also assume that the most male children are born of parents of strong vitality. In the case, where there is definite weakness on one side, then there is possibility of the birth of female child. On a close observation it will be seen that like other States West Bengal consists of majority of agricultural and rural population which mostly depends on physical labour and maintains comparatively good health. It is perhaps one of the reasons that the agricultural and labourer class produce more male children. More females are born of parents, who are naturally weak and lacking in vigour and vitality due to more exercise of brain than that of body. As a result, the gradual decline of female population as a whole is being observed, though there is definite increase of female population among the middle class families.

For a healthy society, there must not exist a wide divergence between the numbers of male and female population as major disharmonies are mostly created by disproportionate sex-ratio. Even the domestic environment, which is of very high significance to the education of a child, is determined to a great extent by this important factor. Sexual promiscuity is regarded in many circles as a social norm since the ideal of virginity is often endangered when this decline of female of population takes an extreme form. Divorces which increase in number due to the above mal-adjustments also mar the integrity of family life. Thus with the moral degeneration of the society, education loses its significance and the social harmony which is the soul of Indian culture begins to shiver. The young learners will then have a tendency to undermine the importance of moral scruple because the ideal of real education and moral training cannot be shown in domestic environment. The narrowness of outlook and undue conservative tendency of people, the racial prejudice and blind faith in customs present some serious problem as well. Like the colour prejudice in America or class distinction in other Western countries, caste system in India with all its false rigidity and narrowness have proved as a definite hindrance to the creation of a progressive society as desired by Raja Ram Mohan Roy, Maharshi Devendranath Tagore, Ram Krishna Paramahansa, Swami Vivekananda and others.

Though modern society has been partly able to propagate the communistic outlook and the principle of equality of right and opportunity through a group of people, still this caste distinction has not yet disappeared from the society particularly of the lower class people. At the same time, a fresh problem has cropped up due to a peculiar class distinction based upon the measure of wealth. The I.A.S. people and those in administrative service form a group whereas the engineers, the doctors have chosen a different group. On the other hand, the middle class mostly comprising petty service holders, *viz.*, clerks, teachers, etc., has a different congregation. In short, the rank consciousness has unfortunately become so prominent now-a-days that the fundamental rights of human beings are even denied and neglected at times.

Therefore, the struggle between the aristocrats and the common run of people, the conflict between the employers and the employees are often found to give rise to different problems mainly due to self-centered outlook. It is the defect in the present system of education and human frailties which presents many other typical problems almost of the same nature, *viz.*, provincialism, religious fanaticism, and communalism. What to speak of the man-made distinctions between people of different religions, different races and creeds or colours, the unfortunate mal-adjustment and misunderstanding even between the people of the same race and nation have made the problem more intricate. Much of the trouble, therefore, is the result of man's incapability of overcoming the prejudices, and narrowness. Prejudice may be compared to a fertile weed, since it grows from the seed of a person's experience and is watered by the imagination of many. These prejudices are often directed against social groups or classes, against nations or against particular religions. Strong nationalism has also been regarded by many philosophers and leaders as a sort of barrier standing on the way to universal love. In this connection, it is worthwhile to remember Rabindra Nath's observations on nationalism where he says that "she has made grave errors in setting up the boundary walls too rigidly between races, in perpetuating in her classifications the results of inferiority. Often she has crippled here children's minds and narrowed their lives in order to fit them into her social forms." This is the problem before us which is the outcome of the creation of imaginary boundary lines between man and man, race and race. Even the discrimination which has been increasing around is proving more harmful in modern times. The male and the female members find it difficult to move smoothly in the life's journey. Series of conflicts often arising between them affect the domestic environment to a great extent. The sacred tie of marriage, the relation between the husband and the wife as instituted in the Hindu society is being challenged. "The chief feature of female life in India is the cultivation of the domestic virtues. All the mental training imparted to them consists of the education received from their mothers which embrace a variety of subjects including religion as well. The principles of propriety and decorum are often instilled into their youthful minds with the greatest care and glimpses of their future destiny communicated to them. The information though given orally, is repeated so often that no part of it fails to make a lasting impression on the mind, and thus the girl learns everything that the mother knows", says some observer. At the same time, it also appears that want of adequate female education is responsible for many problems which have often proved disastrous in social life. Though the conflicts and complexes between the two sexes today are mostly due to misunderstanding, still it can hardly be denied that late marriage and artificial education arc partly responsible for these mal-adjustments.

Thus, it appears that most of the problems, which are mainly due to misunderstanding and conflict, defects in the social structure and human nature, require solution mainly through education. The caste system, the provincialism the racial prejudices, the regional outlook and even the conflict between the sexes have their origin in the mind of the human beings. "A complete freedom from bad habits in individuals, also the freedom from all unclean entanglements may help in holding the banner of civilisation of the future," observes Rabindra Nath in his "Nationalism".

Each individual has his self-love and therefore the instinct of self-preservation leads him to fight with others in the pursuit of his self-interest. It is so natural in human blood that only preaching of abstract ideologies will not help much in the radical cure of these complicated problems. The solution, therefore, should be sought from all sides, economic, social and psychological.

The social structure as it stands today is also seen to exercise enormous influence on the economic life of this land, giving rise to varied problems. For example, we may mention joint family system which in spite of its certain merits has proved unsolvable in the present economic contest. It is generally seen that in a joint family the problem of unemployment, makes its headway and much wastage of energy is caused by callousness and indifferent attitude of most of the young men, who hardly care to earn their own bread. Generally, it is seen that in a joint family one or two members earn whereas many others idle away times in unprofitable pursuits, because they are not forced by circumstances to seek suitable employments. Thus, a few sow the seeds while many others reap the harvest. Often this system gives rise to other types of disputes and undesirable situation in a family as a result of which the relationship between brothers, sisters, uncle and nephew and other relation is unduly strained. This disharmony and strenuous relation, damages the social integrity and affects the healthy family environment. On the other hand, extreme individuality causes many problems as well in family life.

Economic Problems

Problems centre around defects in respect of production, procurement, distribution, consumption, control as well as non-equitable labour.

"Under any economic system there will be a certain amount of stupidity and a certain amount of love of power, each of which will stand in the way of the creation of a perfect educational system," says Bertrand Russell. The influence of economic factors on education is undoubtedly profound and not always superficially obvious. And this influence of economic causes upon education may be dealt with mainly under the following heads:

First is the amount of production which determines to a certain extent the possibility of expenditure for education by the State. It is, therefore, almost certain that in order to improve the system of education and provide opportunities for education to all classes, the State is to depend on the economic resources as well as the amount of production which can be derived from the soil. But as discussed before, it has been seen that the economic position of India particularly in regard to production is far from satisfactory. Therefore, special measures should be taken by the authorities concerned firstly to increase the amount of production by utilising the natural resources man-power as well as the technical aspects of education.

Secondly, the procurement policy is also of vital importance in the field of economics as a satisfactory production does not always ensure a successful procurement and distribution which are most important in the solution of economic problems of a country. It is, therefore, essential that a definite planning should be followed in respect of production, procurement and distribution. In this connection it is worth mentioning that though the State has adopted certain policies in regard to these, still it is of no use denying the fact that the honest intention and the policies of the government have not been fully successful owning to certain apparent defects in their approach to these problems. The food drive, the river projects, the procurement policies a thorough network of civil supplies departments, the rationing system as well as the price-controlling methods are, no doubt, commendable attempts of the State to reach a solution of the varied problems which the country is facing today. But unfortunately enough, most of the measures are not adequate to cope with the intensity and dimension of problems which are making their appearance in bewildering ways. It is not the contention of the present thesis to deal elaborately with economics as well as the laws of production and consumption, and as such, discussion will be directed mainly towards education and psychology. One of the most important developments in the sphere of economic planning has, doubt, been effected by the emergent situation of this land in war-time and particularly in the post-war period. The Second World War was bound to create a series of perplexing problems. The proper solution on the future economic welfare of the country had largely depended on each other. Some of these problems are international and others internal. The most important of these is the sharp rise of the Indian price level and the substantial rise in the cost structure. On the other hand, the internal value of a rupee has undergone a sudden fall followed by the inflation of currency. If we critically look at the very root of the problems it will be observed that war and subsequent conflicts with the neighbouring countries have created evils.

It has inflicted definite injury to mental health of the people, giving rise to most of the evils of the day. Until this can be done away with, no policy of the State in any affair will be crowned with success. Thus we see that every move of the government to solve the economic problems of the country is being faced with crisis due to the dishonest tendency of the people and corruption so strong amongst the mass. It is also surprising that even many government officials have now the least hesitation in taking bribes and other unfair means to fulfill their own interest or selfish motives. These are so common that the attempt of a few to elevate the standard of living as well as to solve the food problems and such other crisis is not coming to any fruition. Besides, difficulties in effecting the policies of procurement and distribution through appointment of procurement officers or rationing system have arisen mainly due to want of co-operative spirit of the public and even their distrust and hostile attitude to these departments. On a close analysis, it will be clear that failure of the government in the task of control. There are certain blunders at its root. Control measures are generally adopted right from the start of the war. In India unfortunately these measures had been adopted only when disruption in the economic structure had already gone too far and the country was engulfed in a vicious circles of conflicts. The social evils and mal-adjustments, the bad social habits cannot be removed overnight. They can be checked and gradually reduced through an evolutionary process by the application of all the social controls, in an effective manner. Amongst the social controls, two types of control will be noticed to render much help. One is more effective such as State, Government or Law implying command, and threats and the other is more spontaneous implying internal force such as public opinion, social evaluation, morality and religion. There are certain evils which have come as a result of reaction against certain undue controls and restrictions such as black-marketing, etc., whereas there are other types of evils which have revealed as natural consequence of heavy economic pressure of life. A different group of crimes and social evils, the seeds of which were sown long ago is also noticed to play very important part in the present society. They are mostly, due to undue oppressions, neglect and contempt of the stronger towards those who were once regarded as weaker and depressed. But the picture has changed today as a result of which much tension and repercussions are making their appearances in very unhealthy manners. The threatening of strike, the riots and such other unorganised revolutions will be seen to have their roots at too deep a level. It is thus seen that unless serious attempts for solution are made primarily through the development of good sense and real education among the people only external controls will do little for permanent check of the evils as well as an effective solution. In short, the problems which are more economic in nature should be solved more by bringing about the desired condition of society through economic uplift and suitable education for the purpose. The problems which are more due to the man-made stratifications and mal-adjustment should be tackled with the joint help of external controls like Law and Government as well as proper education of the mind through ideals and morals.

In India, the competition has so increased, and the social unrest is so strong today that people have lost faith in themselves. They are so much involved for their basic survival that they hardly look after their mental health and moral standards of life. As a result, a neighbour does not hesitate to thrive at the cost of his fellow neighbour, the brother hardly feels any delicacy to encroach upon the legitimate shares of his brother. Thus, the present society of India has almost turned to be a hot bed of chaos and anarchy. All sorts of corruptions which were once not approved by the society have become so common now, that honesty is considered by many as foolishness in the midst of present disruptions. On a critical analysis it will also be observed that with the advent of the new set of problems especially due to displacement of a large group of people, the social structure, the economic position and the cultural heritage of this race have been completely shattered. Majority of the displaced persons are still living in camps completely at the mercy of the government, though a few opportunists are snatching away the lions's share of the government help and thus depriving the real sufferers of their bare necessities. This abnormal situation has unduly exercised its enormous influence not only on society and economic life of the race but also on culture. The most unfortunate thing which has been noticed during this period is that people equally affected have no unity and mutual understanding amongst themselves. It is really surprising that people coming from a particular locality cannot stand his brother sufferers perhaps coming from a different troubled area. It is really painful to observe this disharmony even at the time of a national calamity.

Thus, our society is confronted with the variety of problems having their close bearing on education. One of the major problems in Indian education today is wastage and stagnation at various levels. It is rather depressing that there is a huge wastage of human resources in India partly because we are unable to plan effectively our educational programmes. Very few of those, who take their admission at pre-primary and the primary levels reach the university stage and the number of dropouts at every level of education can hardly be overlooked. In most cases, the sociological reasons dominate over psychological factors. Yet out task is to see how we could bring a social change and promote social welfare through education. The problems of education emerge out of the present social set-up full of unrest and depression. Lack of security among the young generation is one of the outstanding factors contributing to the unrest throughout the country . Similarly, democracy in our country has been recently challenged in manifold ways. Even the behaviour of the responsible persons does not befit his position in many cases and thus we very often hear of crossing the floor in the Parliament or violent agitation here and there for trifling causes. It appears that education has to take a very firm step to bring about a stable atmosphere in this chaotic set-up.

Another common cry of today is that our educational standard is going down. It is rather a delicate task to evaluate educational standard when the base-lines are different but one can easily come to certain generalization. When we try to find an answer to the question, "Is education today meeting the various needs and problems of our changing society?" The answer would be disappointing.

Thus, it seems that the objective we have set-up in our Commission reports are too many and perhaps ambitious. We are, no doubt, aware of the knowledge explosion and imperative need for wider outlook. Yet it becomes very much frustrating if it is experienced that none of the objectives is reached for some reasons or other. Is it the fault of our policy or planning? The question remains to be answered elsewhere.

11

New Perspectives in Education

A Challenge for Education

The role of education for social reconstruction has undoubtedly been demonstrated in various countries at different ages, since time immemorial. Even recently China has brought a social revolution by using education as the main tool. It is, therefore, reasonable to be optimistic about the possibility of using education as a tool for establishing peace and harmony all over the world. Peace is thus a new perspective of education.

Unfortunately, the world today is in the grip of transition. Man of the twentieth century is terribly confused. In spite of that there is a hope that man can modify his nature and adapt himself to the growing demands of time and changing society. Toynbee expresses his optimism and says. "I believe that the human race is going to choose life and good, not death and evil. I, therefore, believe in the imminence of one world, and I believe that in the twenty-first century human life is going to be a unity again in all its aspects and activities."

Much depends upon how we shape up in the context of the nuclear age. It seems obvious that we in India are passing through a critical period. It is not only economy which is dwindling our national life, our values and morality, our cultural heritage are also on the point of fading away. India is a country where peace and harmony have been propagated by a number of illustrious sons of India including Chaitanya and Gandhi. It is the land of Buddha who was an emblem of peace. Yet, we are involved in a heartless struggle and conflict. In society today, human beings no longer meet as friends or companions but solely in the field of struggle for power. Moreover, we as Indians are forgetting our national identity by segregating the entire population into segments and fragments. If harmony is not followed, this small world becomes uncomfortable and modern man becomes miserable. We find that recent years have witnessed much unrest and conflict within nations and races. On the one hand, we are planning space programmes on different planets, while on the other, our motherland is facing violence and disintegration.

Is it then a failure of our modern education to help us in living together with peace and harmony even within the same country and nation?

Thus, we find ourselves at a disadvantage to justify our system of education introduced in free India. It is disheartening to see unrest, confusion and confrontation at all levels of our day-to-day life. We as individuals are emotionally disturbed for reasons not far to seek. Somehow, we are off the balance like boats without anchors. We have lost the tranquillity in our individual life and are subjected to emotional turmoil's. Self-knowledge is almost a myth and knowledge of the matter is gaining prominence. As a consequence, matter and not mind is ruling our day-to-day life. In short, our quest for peace and harmony is being replaced by our passion for power and greed for wealth. Needless to mention that there has been a shift of emphasis in our educational system today from self-knowledge to subject knowledge. The values have changed and our focus has moved to the surface from the centre. One, therefore, wonders as to whether we should revive the old values in our educational system for saving the nation from a total disaster.

Concept of Peace and Harmony

Before planning a comprehensive programme for peace education it is perhaps, logical to analyse the concept of peace. What is peace after all? Thus, peace as a concept needs to be analysed with reference to the purpose. An operational definition of peace may be attempted for working out the procedure for establishing peace. To some, peace is something which is positive, it is not merely avoidance of war. Peace is based on love and caring for others, according to Mother Teresa. Peace is thus a complex and multi-dimensional concept. It has many components and correlates. It involves love and loving. In a sense, peace is a transcendental state of mind, a balanced mental frame with quietness and tranquillity. It also entails a feeling of togetherness and co-existence, affinity and compassion.

There exists a relationship between peace, love, harmony and tranquillity. As mentioned earlier, peace is co-related to progress and advancement toward perfection. In spite of the apparent difference, an operational definition would be helpful for practical purpose. On an analysis of the dimensions of peace, we come to a comprehensive view of peace as an operational concept as follows:

(a) Peace as an internal and inherent mental frame or state.
(b) Peace as a dynamic concept involving interaction.
(c) Peace as a social and political concept implying cessation of hostilities.
(d) Peace as a passive state of non-violence and inaction.
(e) Peace as a concept opposed to war, aggressiveness and hatred.

Peace is, therefore, a complex concept implying love, tranquillity, harmony, mutual understanding, respect and tolerance. It is something more than that. It is equivalent to love, harmony, a positive feeling of oneness with the spirit underlying creation.

Now, the question arises as to how peace can be generated among people, if it is possible to transmit awareness of, and love for peace. It is, however, felt that man is by nature a lover of peace and harmony. At the same time, he is very easily subjected to emotion of hatred leading to violence. The dual forces of love and hatred, of peace and unrest, work within an individual as well as outside at the national and international level. It is the task of education to conquer hatred by love, and unrest by peace. It has also been seen that much of the conflict emerges because of difference in perception. Deeper insight into human nature is possible as a result of love and respect for each individual. Understanding and tolerance are the conditions for creating a climate for peace. Thus, the cognitive processes involved in peace needs to be recognised as well approach to peace education made. Stagner says, "Peace is compatible with human nature and that is why very few people prefer war to peace. Behaviour is a difficult subject-matter not because it is accessible but because it is extremely complex. On the other hand, some idea-affective factor which is clearly a matter, of human values colours our personal feelings, belief and attitude.

On an analysis of the various factors contributing to peace awareness we find that information processing approach to cognition proves effective towards behaviour modification. Much depends upon what kind of experience and information we provide to a child through curricular and co-curricular activities in a school setting. It may be helpful if we organize and re-organize the contents of history, geography, literature and even science in the direction of peace and harmony. The role of a teacher in interpreting facts and contents in the perspective of peace is very significant. Moreover, group discussions, seminars and debates can be significant. Moreover, group discussions, seminars and debates can be organised with a view to reinforcing the concept of peace in the mind of the youngsters. The teacher has a definite role and technique to follow in upholding the value of peace and harmony in the context of culture and humanity. The entire school environment should be conducive to the generation of peace and harmony.

The relationship between the staff-members and pupils should be exemplary and ideal so than it can stimulate desire for peace and love in every mind. Both at the beginning and close of every day school session a prayer and assembly for peace education may be introduced. There should also be regular assemblies for observing special days like human rights days, 'Buddha Jayanti', etc., to encourage the child to grow in the direction of peace and harmony. Similarly, both the staff members and students may be encouraged to organize exhibitions of paintings and sketches on peace. Moreover, special days may be allotted to community and social work to be done by students.

Love, friendship, understanding and mutual respect should characterize the behaviour of both the students as well as the teachers. As mentioned earlier, a comprehensive programme of peace education should be drawn for the entire session so as to incorporate the various dimensions of peace and harmony.

It is thus possible to experiment with the techniques of generating peace among young pupils from the early stages of development. In spite of the importance of cognitive approach to peace education it is felt that the affective domain should also be tapped to reinforce love for peace and harmony in the young mind. Music has a special role in the task of arousing emotions conducive to the generation of peace. Moreover, the behavioural approach may also be attempted, although behaviour is a difficult subject-matter. In other words, behaviour modification has a tremendous scope in the various experiments which may be conducted for the purpose. Suitable environment, social, educational and cultural, may be created to foster the spirit of love and harmony among pupils. Happiness within is a must for social and emotional enrichment. Thus, school as well as home should provide freedom, joy and stimulation for making a child happy. Many studies have demonstrated that substantial differences may occur in the behaviour of the same individual when they are in different situations. For example, children in a democratic system of education grow more socially and emotionally than in an autocratic system. They should be encouraged to share and show concern for others in everyday life in school and outside school. Behavioural science has recently shown increased interest in shaping the environment and it is possible to make an elaborate experiment on behaviour modification. Perception is the process of becoming aware of an environment. Much depends upon how perception and thinking determine our attitude and action. Our perception of reality and environment is influenced by what and how we perceive. According to Skinner, behaviour is shaped and maintained by its consequences. The second result is that the environment can be manipulated in a number of ways.

Concept of National Integration

As discussed earlier, "National Integration" is the beginning of harmony and unity within people. It is essential to have a sense of identity pride and belongingness around the nation one is identified with. National integration demands one-ness a common aspiration and affinity. Motherland should be regarded as no less than mother. All the people belonging to the nation should live and love the country and culture and follow the ethics and principles, the philosophy and goals laid down.

Concluding Observations

A time has come when we should think anew of our educational policy. Although the world today is divided into so many nation states, defined more or less by geographical boundaries and historical traditions, yet people all over the world and human societies have by and large become internationally minded. Science and technology have reduced the distance between one part of the world and the other. An event at any place of the world has its impact on other parts of the world as well. The world has become an organic whole.

Mankind today is moving fast towards its formation of one world family and the people of one part of the world cannot remain indifferent to what is happening elsewhere.

We had previously a more or less settled society and a settled outlook. We formulated our educational policy with reference to our needs and the situation of our society. Our goal was to make our children good citizens who would be physically and mentally fit to move in the world and serve our society and our country well. It is not that these needs have been out of place now. But new responsibilities have been vested in us today and the world situation has changed to such an enormous extent that we are now required to revise the whole perspective.

We have experienced the devastations of two great world wars, and a third one is knocking at the door. It is sure that if a war is fought with the scientific knowledge in our possession, that will lead to annihilation not only of human race, but of the whole civilisation built by the efforts of man for thousands of years. The national rulers of the world are totally indifferent to and oblivious of the great disaster of human race. Hence, the great minds of the world are today crying for a halt to all conflicts and confrontations between nations and nations. We no longer want conflict, but co-operation, not war but peace, not discord, hatred and domination of one nation by another but complete harmony.

But all this requires a complete and total change in the outlook of man, a transformation of character and a sincere real respect for the values of universal brotherhood and unity of man irrespective of caste, creed, religion and geographical and ethnic division. Our children must be taught to be universal men who will break the walls of their social or national ego-centric existence and look upon humanity as tied together by the bonds of unity, justice and brotherhood. We are not educated in that manner, although we have been from time to time confessed about the goal of education. Let us then proceed in a different way. We have thought too much of our society, our state, our nation and, last but not the least, of our personal ends. We have been hardly worldly-wise and practical to be fit for the future world. Let us teach our child that the welfare of his own person is not all, but the well-being of all man, is the goal of his life. Let us remove from his vision all considerations of caste, creed, society, nation and all that divide men geographically, historically, racially and ethnically into fragments. Let us teach our child not to look upon him as Asiatic or European or African and so on. Let him see the world, think for the world and work for the world. The rest will automatically follow. In other words, let there be an education for world peace and not for world war, for harmony and not for discord, for unity and not for division. It is thus that we shall be able to lay the foundation for a new world order and a new world culture, and this is Education for Peace.

12

Education for Emancipation of Creative Consciousness and Inner Harmony

The Modern Orpheus

The modern man is nowhere. His identity—is lost in the doldrums of abstractions and routinised ambiguities, not because he is whipped within but because he is, to coin Rabindranath, 'a torn outline of verse' seeking frantically the strings of harmony within and seeking in vain. A look towards the self is a look towards the self-cemetery. A dead or a cactus land in the desert of desolation: What a modernity? With education continually receding from the worthwhile and invaluable objectives of finding out the man within man and paying for a continual harmony within oneself, the human habitation shamelessly shakes hands with horror and hypocrisy. And the consequence can very well be ascertained. The finer sensibilities and softer emotions of life continually bid farewell from humanity. The unending striving for making the world a very beautiful place to live in and let live others with mutual sympathy, fellow-feeling peace and harmony get a severe jolt only to be mimicried and infatuated with flatteries and affluences born out of the sham exhibitionism in the names of so-called scientific and technological excellences. Who denies that the marvels of civilisation are the endless endeavours for the inner harmony of mankind? The creative consciousness of each and every individual is the creative urge of the human soul. Can this urge be stifled in abstractions forever? But then, the eternal cry within each and every individual to find out the best within him/her withers in the absence of askance in a self-styled prison of passivity's. A modern orpheus, today's individual neither looks at askance for today, nor looks at the past with promises to keep for tomorrow, nor even does he, again, ponder over the possibilities of a better future to forge ahead in fervent hopes and aspirations. The wails within are tears to move nobody, not even himself. The wrinkles on the forehead are so fashioned and fabricated hats off to scientists and technological gadgets that they are no longer the indicators of an unhappy soul. Tears fall only to be soaked in the dust storms of cruelties of passivity's that ignite the fellowmen to recede far and far away till he himself asks: Am I alive?

Objectives

At the outset it should be categorically asserted that at the backdrop of the aforesaid maladies of modernity where creative consciousness and inner harmony of individuality suffer from acute abstractions and passivity's, the following objectives necessitate immediate attention:

(i) to cater in the diverse needs of the individual for enabling him to be equipped with the alertness for his own unique reactions to each and every item contributing to betterment of humanity and strengthening of inner harmony.

(ii) to enable every individual to foster the spirit of self-consciousness and self-creativity leading to enrichment of the human soul.

(iii) to identify and analyse the vulnerable areas of human activities that promote self-growth and self-analysis leading to emancipation of creative consciousness and inner harmony.

(iv) to foster the spirit of looking within and looking askance at one's own self so that it might be possible for one to find out the favourable or unfavourable areas of development of creative awareness and chalk out programmes of activities in accordance with the findings and observations however insignificant those might appear.

(v) to identify and manipulate the catchment areas of creative awareness that more often than not are not given any importance in the diffusion of a generalised stream of thoughts and activities affecting freedom to grow and freedom to be as one should be.

(vi) to look into an individual's peculiar avenues of creative consciousness so that identification, analysis and synthesis of the positive points of individual potentiality might be worthily and most satisfactorily geared to promotion of inner harmony.

(vii) to enkindle the spirit of inner worth of every individual in accordance with the felt needs and priorities to be given weightage.

(viii) to identify and analyse the abstractions and anomalies that stand in the way of efflorescence of an individual's creative sensibilities.

(ix) to enable an individual to suggest by himself the probable avenues of his own inner harmony however little it might be felt.

(x) to identify and analyse the operational avenues of an individual's creative consciousness and inner harmony.

The Perfume of Promise

The education that is of utmost importance for an individual is to grow within and to enrich the finer sensibilities and softer visions of life. The world as it is necessitates for him to develop deep into the wonderland of feelings and trends of thoughts that react most thrillingly with variations of imagery patterns. For this he requires self-training, through maintenance of balance and harmony of his reactions for different and diverse antecedents awaiting new and wider veils of efflorescence and emancipation. Perhaps herein lies the difference between man and man a difference that is the consequence of uniqueness that must, at all cost, be maintained and must be allowed to be nurtured and thrived as and when an individual desires according to his own whim and temperaments. The world of free discipline thus gets a wider perspective of emancipation.

And when, from the above viewpoint, education beckons a promise of self-development and self-activity, it also ensures the fact that all education is, in the end, an education for self-consciousness, self-creativity and ceaseless pursuit for inner harmony. The awakening of creative consciousness is the green signal that an individual receives along with the operation of educational orientations taking place intrinsically or extrinsically. The only caution to be taken against anomalies in educational operations is to see whether the successive steps for self development and self-activity are really leading to a synchronized outcome of creative consciousness — a fact, also, sand witched in and throttled up in a mess of multiplicities of scientific and technological bangs.

Admittedly, the man within man is lost in the melee of dittos and proxies. But who denies the boundless sky of the mind of an individual?

Who can step aside from the unparalleled awe and agonies of the human soul? The search for synchronization even in apparent balance and harmony is again, not the last world of human excellences to be so cheaply lost in happy-go statistical acrobatics of evaluation. The evaluation of man is directed towards eternal flight of birds of the perfumes of promise so characteristically remarked by Rabindranath. Agonies arrived at and experienced are agonies for betterment of 'I' — the ceaseless breaker of all norms of human potentiality and creative consciousness.

> This is my delight, thus to wait and watch
> at the wayside where shadow chases light
> and the rain comes in the wake of the summer.
>
> Messengers, with tidings from unknown
> skies, greet me and speed along the road,
> My heart is glad within, and the breath
> of the passing breeze is sweet.
>
> From dawn till dusk I sit here before
> my door, and I know that of a sudden the
> happy moment will arrive when I shall see.

> In the meanwhile I smile and I sing all
> along. In the meanwhile the air is filling
> with the perfume of promise.
>
> — Gitanjali [XLIV]

The sense of delight seeking deliverance from the routine-oriented craze of dutifulness awaits the beckoning of moments of newer ecstasies, the consciousness in creative thinking being thus ready for a newer journey to seek delight in the harmony within refreshed and re-enkindled for a better promise of performance. The aroma of excellence comes out of the blooming mind — the joy of the mind sailing through the sea of imaginations sweeping over the web of ideas.

The Education of 'Being'

The highest education awaiting emergence and inculcation of autology presupposes the heightening and endless re-orienting of creative consciousness and inner harmony. The 'cetasa' must broaden and enlighten 'cidakas', the sky of the mind. For this the education of being, of self-identification, is yet to usher forth in brilliance and lustre. Perhaps education misinterprets science or *vice versa* but that is entirely an outcome of our camouflaged vision of life lost in living. Meanwhile, the modern Orpheus is frantically expectant of the notes of optimism. Why not allow him to look back within with the words of a great creative genius?

> The song that I am to sing remains unsung
> to this day.
> I have spent my days in stringing and in
> unstringing my instrument.
> The time has not come true, the words have
> not been rightly set: only there is the
> agony of wishing in my heart.
> The blossom has not opened: only the
> wind is sighing by.
>
> (Rabindranath Tagore: Gitanjali, xiii)

The following are the correlates of creative consciousness:

1. an attitude of 'live and let live';

2. respect for others' views and tolerance;
3. a conviction that 'all human being are equal'
   in addition to
   (a) general knowledge;
   (b) proficiency in the application of knowledge; and
   (c) critical thinking.

and other personality qualities. Now this is again the question of values which would determine the issue. The question will remain unanswered until the criterion in terms of value is fixed up. This will remain a controversy as will be evident from few observations. Sardar Panikar, formerly Vice-Chancellor of the University of Mysore, observed that the standard of education in the country had not fallen as alleged by some people, but had gone up, while Sri Prem Kripal has indirectly supported the hypothesis that our educational standards are falling at certain levels in certain respects. So far as standards at university level are concerned, the same controversy would persist. The problems may vary in dimensions, but fundamentally most of them are alike.

There are various dimensions of educational standard. The continuous change in the composition of various factors of education stands on the way of any sound comparison. Curriculum, teachers, methodology, evaluation, etc., are changing in a dynamic set-up. In spite of the fact that all the changes are affected for the sake of betterment of standards, there is a growing dissatisfaction with the present educational standard. It may be that this feeling is partly due to emotional attachment with the impression 'when we were young'. But is it the only reason?

There may be another possibility that the modern age has the highest demands on our education with the expanding frontiers of knowledge. In that case, we will have to survey our various needs and evaluate the educational standard with reference to each of the needs forming the criteria.

This seems to be a better proposition. Instead of trying to compare standards at two different periods, it would be perhaps more worthwhile to investigate into our present emerging needs as well as outstanding values in life, and plan our educational programme to meet those adequately. It would be a wild goose chase, if we fail to control the variables of background before comparing on an objective basis. Whether our educational standards are falling or not, would thus remain a subjective and debatable question, unless adequate data could be collected and interpreted with scientific precision. There is, of course, a general consensus that we are gaining more and more in range and less and less in depth.

There is a strong feeling that students today are more informed and less thorough, more sensitive but less critical, more distracted and less concentrating or persistent.

So far as the values of life are concerned, the picture appears to be blurred by so many images. It appears that the present student population tends to be less introspective with varied interests, more pragmatic and confused and less interested in knowledge for the sake of knowledge. These are, however, some of the general impressions formed by a particular group of thinkers.*

It is indeed a gratifying phenomenon that 'old order change the yielding place to new', but it reflects a fluctuating tendency. When one sits to examine the oft-quoted statement beginning with 'old is gold' on the one hand, and 'new is noble', on the other extreme, it leads us nowhere, if we merely continue to relish the past glory and condemn the new change. Similarly, it is equally stagnating if we close our eyes to the past and fail to evaluate the change with reference to the emerging values of life. The values of life are unfortunately at cross-roads. It is thus essential to determine the values in order of priority before undertaking any other exploration of this nature.

* Acknowledgement: Contributed by Sri Mohit Kumar Chakrabarty in the journal New Perfectives edited by the author.

13

Education for Peace

"Wars start in the minds of men", declares the U.N. Charter. Therefore, peace is a state of mind. It is this state of mind which is claimed to be moulded by education. It is theoretically possible to have a state of mind full of peace even amidst the heat of war. This applies equally to individuals, communities, and nations. Conceptually peace is anti-war, anti-destruction. It is also a positive attitude without reference to war. Peace is anti-competition and pro-cooperation. This is the societal aspect of life. However, it is possible to retain a state of positive competition while pursuing excellence as is the case of the wrestler in a ring. They have nothing against each other. They are supposed to be fighting to prove the superiority of a particular style or approach to fighting. If this is extrapolated to all healthy competitions, any competition can be peaceful. However, a lot can be said of human mind conducive to peace for inculcating this attitude. What are the factors associated with peace? Who are the persons responsible for generating peace? These are some of the questions that bother the educationists today.

Peace has become a crucial issue in the present state of the world where the entire humanity is threatened with a total annihilation. It is said that at present there is so much stockpile of nuclear weapons that the world can be finished within minutes. The entire control of these weapons is also under the power of some individual nations. There is presently no indication of solution to this problem. Human efforts to bring down the mental state of aggression among those powers building-up lethal weapons have not succeeded in such a manner that the planet can feel secure for even another hundred years.

The lesson for education for peace will have to be drawn from different sources. One of the most powerful sources will certainly be the texts of different religions. Apart from their differences in details and approaches to life we can be sure that all religions were meant to help man's survival, to help inculcate the habit of loving other human beings rather than hating them and to strive for a better harmony and better spiritual contentment. If we forget that part of religions which indulged in conflicts by initiating competition with other religions and generating hatred and look at the basic messages of the religions, perhaps the scriptures and texts will tell us a different story. It should also be remembered that the texts written centuries earlier will have to be interpreted in the context of the present and immediate future. These interpretations will also have to be unbiased and devoid of selfishness or propagation of one ideology or the other. The validity of those portions of the texts which referred to the narrow concept of communities, taboos and customs at the time of their writing will have to be ignored. Admittedly this is going to be a difficult task and may require sophisticated team-work and conceptual philosophical exercises of the highest order. Fortunately, persons like Vivekananda, Rabindranath Tagore and Mahatma Gandhi had attempted to bring about integration of different religious thoughts in this country in the modern century. Earlier we find works of Guru Nanak, the Sufi saints and others which may be of great help.

The next part of the lesson will have to be drawn from the history of human cultures and civilizations. If one studies the causes of human conflicts and their consequences, it is likely that the significance and relevance of peace will be revealed. Obviously this cannot be done all at once. Neither is a human child capable of absorbing these messages of complex nature at an early stage. On the other hand, if the message is given through pedagogical principles gradually building-up as the child grows, it will lead to greater maturity and real attitudinal development. The messages, of course, will have to be drawn from authentic sources and interpreted in an unbiased way, without any adverse remarks against any human community. This also requires a sophisticated conceptual exercise. This has also been fortunately interpreted by great thinkers like Toynbee and Nehru. These interpretations can be easily built into the standard curriculum of history. It can also be discussed separately in the context of literature, philosophy and social studies.

Auxiliary sources like human geography, economics, anthropology and linguistics can be helpful in re-interpreting the causes and consequences of various fluctuating tendencies among different human societies. The insight into such past conflicts may help in preventing similar instances for similar issues. It is also likely that the learner would see the shallowness, of such conflicts. It requires the same unbiased objectivity as in the case of religion or history. Unfortunately such exercises have not been attempted directly. There may be many other sources from different social sciences which can be brought into consideration for studying such conflicts. At the same time stories of communities which have learnt to live in peace and have learnt to resolve conflicts nicely within themselves will have to be focussed.

Whenever one thinks of education, one thinks of the teacher. The role of the teacher in education for peace will have to be delineated somewhat independent of the context of subject, matter and methods. When it is a question of bringing out attitudinal and emotional changes and not merely academic attainments, the teacher must learn to handle the emotions of his pupils, to adjudicate the conflicts among them. In the attitudinal plane, the human mind can be extremely sensitive. One careless statement or a slip may cause havoc in the pupil's mind. It is here that the significance of moral education reveals itself in the context for peace and harmony. Moral education aims at self-disciplined orderliness in thought and restrain in emotions. The teacher should not only impart the above lessons from the religious texts, history and other auxiliary sources but also must be capable of showing both by examples and precepts the significance of such lessons.

The parents and members of the communities around the school are also equally responsible for shaping education for peace. One cannot have a peaceful educational institution amidst a non-peaceful society. One cannot imagine full success of education for peace without reinforcement from the community. Ideally this will call for a total social change. At the same time, we cannot wait for such a revolution before beginning our attempt for education for peace. The community is even slower than the child learning the lessons for peace. If the teacher changes his role as an organiser, as a perceiver and preceptor, then perhaps the community will start responding. Such ideal things have happened in this country when saints started teaching about life in their monasteries. While it is too much to expect saintliness from each teacher, a modest beginning among teachers will be quite rewarding. Apart from the role of the teacher, the environmental changes required for an atmosphere of peace within the school will have to be properly thought of. This may include changes in the co-curricular activities, portraying of great champions of peace, reading and discussion of their life and philosophies, etc. Education for peace will be a product of many processes and multi-dimensional endeavours.

In view of the factors discussed above a tentative model for education for peace may be presented. It is being proposed to add a few more factors into the model which have obvious significance for peace in education. The position of the person is central to the model because education purports to address only individuals and the effects on the community, society, nation and the world are supposed to be consequential. Peace, which is the consequence, is interlinked in the process. This simply means that it can be interpreted both as a process and a product.

A TENTATIVE MODEL FOR PEACE

Lessons from the Past

Education.....................

Faith Morality Non-aggression

Positive Attitude	World (W)	Nation (N)	Society (S)	Comm-unity (C)	Indivi-dual	(C)	(S)	(N)	(W)	Emo-tio-nal Bala-nce
	Integration			Peace					Tolerance	

Education.......................... Present awareness
Threats from Future

14

Education for Harmony

Harmony is a co-ordinated and integrated progress towards the same goal. When the progress obeys a system helpful to the generation of relations and evolution of a higher order of integration it becomes harmony. In each aspect of life and life-function there are obviously many elements each of which changes. Where the change and rate of change of different elements obey the same rhythm they contribute towards the progress of the whole. They evolve a harmony.

Life in itself is an organismic function. It is a growth towards a higher order of relations with the different environments. Progress or growth is a change in two different ways. While one way of change is horizontal expansion of relations the other way is a change from a lower order to a higher order. Expansion in relations of the same order at any level is also diverse. It is a common observation that when a person becomes inclined to a set of specific relations he neglects the other aspects of relations. The balance in life-relations is lost. He gradually develops a maladjustment and progress comes to almost a stop. Life becomes a monotone, dull, mechanical existence. The cause is a loss of harmony. On the other hand, if relations are multiplied at any level without an integration, a disorder leading to a chaotic condition sets in and progress slows down.

When an attempt is made in evolving a higher order of integration without growth in all the aspects of life, integration fails. Progress in any one or more aspects of growth is possible but it does not lead to a stabler and more integrated life. Life becomes a void. The cause is again a loss of harmony.

Like the individual life, social life is also a growth in two ways. One is the expansion of interpersonal and inter-group relations and the other is the progress of human civilization and culture from a lower order of integrated organisation to a higher order of integrated organisation of the world society.

Interpersonal relations may take three different forms — a relation bringing the two together, a relation where the two moves almost parallel to each other, each without any concern about the other and the third one moving away from the other. Symbolically, if the first one is positive, the second one is zero or null and the third one are negative. The first set of interpersonal relations generates a co-operative society leading to social integration, while the third set generates a competitive society leading to social exploitation and disintegration, a sign of lack of harmony.

Without the evolution of a higher order of integrated organisation a gathering of persons functions without a specific goal. This again is the syndrome of a loss of social harmony.

Like all essential variables of life, harmony is also universal in distribution. No entity is found without the least harmony whether internal or external and no entity is possible in the fullest harmony with this word of substance. The second important characteristic is that lesser harmony can generate harmony through purposeful endeavour.

It is clear that greater harmony is manifested in two aspects of life both internal and external. Harmony in the external relations is manifested in organisation and harmony in internal relations is manifested in integration.

Harmony in external relations is evolved through the committed acceptance of a specific value-system or of value-systems similar to one another. Harmony in internal relations is evolved through a growth of the mind through its different phases.

A continuum of variation may be realised from disharmony to harmony through compromise. It is told that life is a set of compromises. Through compromise one can gradually move towards full harmony. It is also realised by intuitive realises that Nature is moving through compromises towards harmony.

Education is claimed to be a process of purposeful interaction pointing to an immediate target and a remote goal. Even if the ultimate product of all interactions be realised to be harmony, a set of interactions may bring out a set of immediate products which retard the growth towards the ultimate.

Educational systems have been evolved in some cases with the immediate targets or objectives in view, in other cases keeping the ultimate in view. It has been found that even though these systems have proved to be effective in many respects, these have often failed to evolve a greater harmony.

Assuming harmony as a mental attribute or psychological organisation, manifested in behaviours the reverse has been postulated to be valid, *viz.*, practice of a set of physical-physiological and mental-emotional behaviours lead to the development of a conceptual frame of behaviours and ultimately, generates a value-system in the individual. This system being stably established determines the motives underlying all behaviours internal and external, individual and social.

Thus, it becomes imperative that a set of behavioural practices be determined which evolve from a value system which is in concordance with harmony. A programme may be set within a controlled environment to provide a sequential practice of behaviour synchronised with the natural growth.

Through the empirical reflective researches in psychology and education it has been found that cognition, concept, formation, evaluation, appreciation and creation are the hierarchical phases of growth functions. However hierarchical, they evolving in nature and as such in some form or other operate simultaneously. So in the education process, the scope for their functioning is to be provided. A two-way consideration with the accepted value-system of impersonal relations, growth and expansion both in time and space is useful for the development of the educational programme.

Age-grouping	Years				
Ed. function Life needs behavioural	0-3	3-6	6-10	10-14	14-12
Social Interaction					
Cognitive Development					
Appreciation Development					
Psychical Development					
Creative Development					

ENVIRONMENT — RESPONSIVE AND CO-OPERATIVE

A responsive environment is a constructed controlled environment where sufficient stimulus can be provided for the child to interact and respond. Where attention and scope is provided to respond to free and divergent stimuli from the child, where scope is provided for the child to share external stimulation, interaction, actions and responsibilities with co-operating adults. The adults are to seek co-operation from the child, utilize it and co-operate in their functions.

The programme is to be constructed in such a way that from the very beginning a harmonious growth is fostered through living a life based on harmony. The child is to be so habituated to a harmonious life that he can sense the lack of harmony, be dissatisfied, locate the causes of dissatisfaction and try to remove it.

The programme may be organised with the local resources available and so a stereotyped curriculum is not appropriate.

A system of evaluation may be inbuilt within the programme to assess the growth of each individual in each aspect. The evaluation is to be criterion-based instead of a norm-based one. The criteria are growth manifestations.

Teachers dedicated to the cause may gradually develop their competency. As a well-beaten path is not available, adequate and persisting research is to be carried on for evolving the alternate programmes on education as well as teacher-preparation.

15
Education for Survival

Man today is terribly confused and confronted with a number of problems. It is surprising that in modern society human beings no longer meet as friends or companions but solely in a field of struggle for power. As Margaret Mead remarks, "We have segregated the entire population into segments, into fragments so that nobody has a whole experience. If this is reality, then indeed modern man is the poorest creature in the entire universe." In fact, very little is being accomplished with regard to the greatest problem of our day, the threat of nuclear war. Our survival is at stake and the possibility of annihilation of mankind is not very remote.

On a critical study of human conflicts it appears that war is in our blood as conflict lies in human nature. In spite of the bitter experiences of the past, we may not have learnt much from the history of mankind. Is it not strange that man has not yet been able to win over his inner nature, his frailties and frivolities although he has made remarkable progress in technology and science. The psychological forces still remain unconquered. Our education is causing knowledge explosion but not the integration of the propensities in human nature. An effective planning for avoiding the impending disaster demands education for survival, education for harmony, and peace. It is obvious that the modern education is hardly balanced to contribute to the total growth of man. For reasons not far to seek, the cognitive area of human development is stressed. As a result, man is heading with a passion toward knowledge of facts and not the ultimate truth. Unfortunately, mere accumulation of information in various disciplines is receiving priority.

Even the knowledge of the method of science is not helping children much toward perception of absolute reality in human nature. Indeed education has a great responsibility to provide the basic understanding of the world affairs as well as the reality we live in today. Advance in social sciences including education is yet to be made to strike at the very root of the problems around conflicts of all types. On the one hand, human aggression is to be accepted as a reality, while on the other, education has to be geared to the purpose of channelizing or sublimating our emotions. A study of the dynamics of hostility reveals that energy mobilization, if confined and unsuccessful to meet a challenge, tends to flow out into destructive channels. In this way, the inner hostility affects and distorts perception through projection.

The purpose of this paper is to deliberate on the possibilities of engaging education and relevant techniques for developing every conceivable aspect related to the survival of mankind. No doubt, the problems facing mankind today are of varied dimensions which should be attacked in a number of ways both educationally as well as socially. Besides, the psychological approach to conflict resolution is relevant to the purpose.

Let us first concentrate on education as a tool for bringing the desired result, *i.e.*, the survival of mankind from all kinds of disasters. As an agent of social change as well as a social control, education has tremendous potential to meet the challenges from physical, political, religious and socio-economic environment. Education, in all its perspectives, holds promise to cope with some of the vital issues concerning humanity today.

The various frontiers of knowledge have to be opened along with a vigorous attack on the inherent weakness of human nature. It would be, perhaps, relevant to mention here that a man's behaviour or even a group behaviour is determined not only by what he thinks but also what and how he feels. In other words, the affective domain has to be brought to bear upon the cognitive process underlying group behaviour. Moreover, the emotions which play vital roles behind human behaviour have to be handled properly for maximizing the role of perception and reasoning in the context of psychological reality.

It is possible to shape the attitude of human beings by reinforcing the perception, although it is difficult to handle the aggressive tendencies of human beings in an experimental way. It is experienced that an aggressive behaviour may be the outcome either of hatred or of expression of anger. Moreover, war has become a source of excitement, a liberating experience to many. In other words, the appeal of war is too profound to be neutralized by sensible arguments of rational men. Thus activities of war and international hostilities can be viewed as a series of inter-related paradoxes.

Education for harmony and peace depends upon the positive concept of peace. A desire for peace has to be generated in the minds of the people at large. In fact, various approaches may be made available not only for resolution of conflicts but also for creating a climate for peace and international understanding. Education in every sense of the term can be employed for promotion of human living and functioning.

Man has been intrigued by his own misdeeds and misjudgments resulting in the ecological imbalance and pollution of all kinds. It is rather strange that the technological and scientific education man is receiving to-day is at this stage of little help for his meaningful survival. It is tragic to go against the delicate balance in environment maintained by nature. Very little concern for harmony, happiness and humanity is shared by the nations and their leaders. Human nature is too complex to be manipulated in a planned direction. This is why the cognitive approach to survival of mankind is not proving very effective. In order to tap the functions and the unconscious domains guiding human behaviour, various methods and techniques are to be adopted. Of them the following deserves special mention:

1. Formulation of goals and objectives in terms of the well-being of mankind.
2. Developing educational programmes for betterment of world situation, self-fulfillment and social uplift.

The concept of survival of mankind is changing with the expanding horizon of human experience. It is not only the pollution of the environment or the ecological imbalance which is disturbing the present generation of man, the main threat of the catastrophe comes from the internal conflict within man, the basic contradictions in human nature. Thus we find conflicts and war at various levels over the globe at certain intervals. Besides, the natural resources are being over-exploited causing an imbalance in ecology. Similarly, in the social context we find lots of unrest and tension, crimes and anti-social activities. These are the most outstanding menaces of man to-day. Survival of mankind is, therefore, dependent upon the remediation of the maladies described above.

The various dimensions of the survival problems are more conspicuous today than ever, mainly because of men's ignorance, indifferences and lack of concern. In addition, man has to learn from his mistakes about the drastic reaction of nature if over-exploited. It is thus imperative to educate people, specialists and readers to help them to ensure environmental protection and maintain ecological balance. With a view to promoting the understanding of environment in relation to man, a systematic programme should be developed. The approaches should be made in all directions including development of materials, tests and projects at all levels for generating the awareness of the need for protecting environment. Mass media of communication should be used for educating public in an informal way, so that steps are taken to prevent deforestation as well as air and water pollution. Some kind of attitude and outlook must be developed toward better living and harmonious functioning. As human mind is a frail instrument mere awareness and cognitive approach would be far from being effective. What is needed is the reinforcement of the balanced perception of reality and a zeal for meaningful life. In spite of the constant turmoil's and havocs going on in the history of human race, Toynbee has expressed his optimism in the future of mankind when he says, "I believe that the human race is going to choose life and good, not death and evil". In spite of the inherent goodness within man the world today is being plundered and mishandled. It is the irrational man, who is responsible for the present crisis.

In fact, problems will pile up until man will wake up to reality and start searching within him the reason for his failure to live together on earth with harmony and happiness. His quest will be primarily a moral quest seeking the foundation on which a morality for a new age can be established. It is not merely the lack of vision which is responsible for this crisis and confusion, it is the lack of determination and goodwill which is absolutely essential for a better world. One of the values of living in a transitional age *i.e.*, an age of therapy, is that it forces the opportunity open for us to uncover new meaning in perennial man to see more deeply into his own nature.

As mentioned earlier, the approaches to all the problems enumerated before should be not only cognitive, they should be practical and experimental as well. Right from the very childhood, education should be oriented to the need for harmony and happiness for humanity at large. The educational programme should be drawn up to attack the various problems including confusion, inertia, prejudice and lack of proper attitude.

It is interesting to observe that people are not fully aware of the direction in which they are going and it is likely that they will awaken when it is too late and when the fate has been irrevocably sealed. Yet the history of man is, however, a history of growing awareness and, in spite of the tragic disproportion between intellect and emotion in our society today, man is perhaps at the beginning of the process of discovery of his limits and limitations.

It is indeed uncertain as to whether the destructive power which his present knowledge has given him will permit him to improve his life-style for peace and harmony or whether he will destroy himself before he can build-up a fuller picture of reality on the present foundation. Man has not only his head, he has also the heart. The reason why he is mysterious is that in his nature lies a bundle of paradoxes. He is individual yet, social, unified yet diversified, complete yet incomplete. He finds meaning through cognition, yet he is often guided by his emotions. Margaret Mead asks a very pertinent question with deep concern for mankind, "Are we trapped, not by a set of innumerable instincts which determine that we will in all cases turn to aggression and exploitation of others when we are strong enough?" She suggests a very realistic and at the same time dispassionate solution by saying that one of the essential elements in escape from an infinitely greater threat is the willingness to acknowledge that our know-how, is not enough.

On a critical study of the forces behind the problem of human survival, it would appear that the most outstanding problem is that of perception and perspective. They are important because without the right type of perception our knowledge of the entire perspective of man is failing to meet the challenge of his survival. His added knowledge of science and technology in isolation is not helping him much to live happily together on this beautiful planet.

It is, however, paradoxical to think that the civilized man of this scientific age is hopelessly dabbling into politics, pollution and prejudice.

Is it not a tragedy that man is standing at the place he was at the beginning, helpless and trapped by psychological barriers? On the one hand, he is trying to win over the challenges of nature, while on the other he is ruining the delicate balance prevailing in nature by his adamant spirit of exploitation. In fact, his knowledge of matter is not adequate as his ignorance of the art of harmonizing the matter with the spirit of nature is colossal.

As suggested in the *UNESCO* publication (No. 22) on "Education for International Understanding", in teacher-education the importance of adding a global perspective to various studies is emphasized. For example, science would deal with global concerns like disarmament, pollution and diminishing resources such as oil, farm-lands and water. Other subjects like the social studies would consider and evaluate national and international efforts to deal with such problems. Thus curriculum should be developed in an integrated manner to deal with the problem of human survival and teachers should learn to direct the subject knowledge to the relevant ends. In other words, catering information should not be the only goal of education. Both teachers and students are made aware of the need for processing and interpreting the information in the context of human survival. Besides instructional methods, creative teaching should be introduced at all levels to generate the sensitivity and awareness needed in each area as well as to challenge the creativity, imagination and resourcefulness of the learners. For example, children of various ages may be encouraged to make artistic presentation of their perception of peace, ecological balance and use or misuse of energy. Paintings and art-work, depicting the outcome of war or abuse of natural resources as well as pollution may have impact on the mass-consciousness. Films, slides, radio or television broadcast and other innovative materials may be effective for creating a suitable climate for reinforcing perception and attitude formation. Obviously simultaneous attacks should be made at both the cognitive and affective levels for directing appropriate behaviour for survival of mankind.

Particularly in teacher-education programme attempt should be made to create and strengthen programmes, designed to promote international education by creating favourable conditions with materials, organisation and support-measures; appropriate to the task. Besides the institutionalized programmes, the following may be organised for orientation to the basic issue for human survival:

(a) Regular courses for cross-cultural studies in different subject areas.
(b) Frequent exchange of visits, study-tours, etc.
(c) Organisation of seminars on different topics around human survival.
(d) Organizing regular radio and broadcasting programmes on different cultures and various issues including environmental protection, use and abuse of natural resources as well as various types of energy.
(e) Intensive research on the modalities of perception of physical social and cultural environment in international context.
(f) Organising international exhibition for displaying the various art materials including painting, sketches, sculpture, music or poetry for creating impact on the affective domain.
(g) Manipulating human resources for focussing on the relevant issues even by using mass-media or audio-visual materials.

Regarding the problems of disarmament, it has been found that a feeling of insecurity and fear, stands on the way to the sincere effort for arms reduction. While one speaks of disarmament, nuclear weapons pile up. A lack of mutual trust and confidence always hinders any progress towards peace. It is extremely difficult to get rid of the distrust and apprehensions for generating a climate conductive to peace. Various types of experiments may be conducted for exploring the possibility of reduction of distrust and fear. Even therapeutic measures are recommended for the leaders to help them in coming out of the paranoid state of mind.

Experimental approaches have been made to explore the possibility of arousing typical emotions by means of specific stimuli or a combination of them. It has been observed that in most cases fear and a feeling of insecurity lead to aggressive designs, resulting in atrocities. With a view to generating the trust and confidence, the basic feeling of security should be instilled not by accumulation of destructive weapons but through psychological methods of interaction. It is very often observed that real war starts after the psychological warfare for a while. Either ego or pride and prejudice provoke warfare and hostilities at every level.

In conclusion, it can be said that human survival demands the potential to face the challenges of life as well as man's capacity for manipulation of environmental resources with a definite purpose in view. In every case there are problems both organisational as well as human. And the task of education is to offer the key to the solution of those problems. In the real sense of the term education has manifold functions including planning and programming in the right direction.

The fate of the world rests on two assumptions:

1. That carefully selected man will retain cool judgment during an intense conflict; and
2. That even if one man fails others will act as a 'fail-safe' device.

It is, however, doubtful if these assumptions are correct in all contexts. Many of our social problems today may not reach easy solutions. Nevertheless a science of peace has to be developed for solving our current social problems by way of scientific psychology and analysis.

Education for living in harmony with happiness for humanity is the top priority today.

References

1. Angell, Norman, *The Great Illusion,* New York. G. P. Pitmans, 1813.
2. Berkowit, Leonard, *Roots of Aggression,* New York, Atherton Press, 1955.
3. Boulding, K. F., *Peace and the War Industry,* Chicago, Aldine Publishing Co., 1971.
4. Bhattacharya, S., *Dynamics of Human Emotions and World Peace,* Book Land, Calcutta, 1972.
5. Delhers, K. H, *Conflict Measurement by the Dynamic Calculus Model and its Application to Clinical Practice*, Multivariate Research, Special Issue, 1968.
6. Mead, Margaret, *Culture and Commitment,* New York, Doubleday and Co., 1970.
7. Nityaswarupanand, Swami, *School of World Civilization,* Calcutta R. K. Mission, 1967.
8. Rogers, C. R. and Steavens, Barry, *Person to Person,* California, Real Press, 1967.
9. Skinner, B. F., *Beyond Freedom and Dignity,* New York, Bantam Books, 1971.
10. Stangner, Ross, *Psychological Aspects of International Conflict,* California, Brooks/Cole Publishing Co., 1969.
11. Bhattacharya S., *Long Road to Peace,* Vantage Press, 1977.
12. Bhattacharya S., *Peace and War,* Liberty Press, Michegon U.S.A.

16

Education for International Understanding

Education has been considered as an effective means for bringing any change in the attitude, skill and behaviour of people. It has been regarded as a social control by Butrand Russel.

The world today is in the grip of transition. As it is shrinking every day, the entire human family has to learn to live in harmony and peace.

Education for international understanding has become for human survival.

Nothing can save mankind from total disaster unless a peace climate is created and the leaders can be influenced in formulating a policy of disarmament.

This is not an easy task and attempts are being made certain quarters to create a world opinion against war.

There are of course long-term preventive measures and more constructive steps to ensure peace and harmony in the world. The most effective way is to generate a desire for peace and harmony at every level in the Society.

There are various approaches to peace education and more peace studies are needed to discover effective ways to handle human conflicts at all levels.

Promotion of International understanding is one of those describing special mention.

UNESCO's attempt to promote international understanding at schools through education may be mentioned in this connection.

There are even recommendations to start fostering the spirit of harmony and peace among children at the Primary and pre-primary level.

Children are our future hope. Montessori has rightly said, "Establishing peace is the work of education". The child in her view, is to be seen as a "Savior capable of regenerating the human race and society".

Besides, the rapid extension or the various forms of mass communication, seems to bring education a new dimension. Mass communication tends to reinforce common symbolic systems, to enrich, re-express and re-interpret them. The school must share its monopoly of education with the Institution responsible for communication.

The impact of educational action of the media on cognitive development or behaviour is obvious.

Much depends upon the psychological intellectual, social and cultural conditions of the individuals exposed to them. From this point of view, interpretation of the non-formal education of the media is undergoing the same change as thinking on education.

Emphasis is to be laid on the role of interpersonal relations and the influence of the values.

There has been discourse and discussion on the emergence of a new man whom this new environment could in varying degrees fashion front day-to-day. The emotional contexts and his habits of reasoning, his critical attitudes and imagination, his technical skills and behaviour are to be taken into account.

Up until the beginning of this century, the functions of the school and those of the family have been considered very important, although the growing presence of communication in the most Societies raise the question of re-appraisal of the function of the School.

Some pragmatists hold that the communication media should purveys contemporary knowledge, while education should be responsible for passing on the heritage accumulated by tradition.

Thus, the school and the communication as a system should supplement each other in carrying out their responsibilities for promotion of international understanding.

The schools at all levels should think in terms of education of children to help them to love and live in harmony and peace to understand and respect other cultures and to become a worthy citizen of the world.

The role of the schools is changing considerably with the changing time. Education for survival is the top most priority. The schools as well as other institutes of culture should develop the programmes, curricular and co-curricular according to the basic needs for human survival.

Need for Peace Education and Peace Studies in Indian Context:—

With a view to promoting peace education in India, a comprehensive Programme has to be set up for attacking the different dimensions of peace education.

Accordingly, attempts are being made by the author of this paper to establish an Association or Society for Peace Education in India to set up Programme of activities as follows:

1. To promote Peace Studies in India.
2. To disseminate Peace Education in the Community.
3. To instill Peace and International understanding in the minds of School going Children.
4. To set up a model child development institute for experimentation and approaches to peace education.

Conclusion

The concept of Peace is multi-dimensional. It has implications and applications much wider than anticipated; that peace is within may be realized in any individuals life through harmony.

It may be cultivated and generated at various levels including individual and group, national and international.

In the present decade, the entire humanity is threatened with the probability of a nuclear war. Behind this, lies, ignorance and prejudice, intolerance and hatred.

With a view to establishing peace at all levels both preventive and curative measures, have to be adopted. A strong faith in peace and harmony, an urge for international understanding should be instilled in the minds of the people including children, our future hope.

There is also a scope for research on the nature of materials to be used and techniques applied for peace-education.

The general aim of establishing this association is to generate and promote peace, harmony and international understanding at various levels.

With a view to formulating specific objectives of Peace Education for International Understanding an advisory committee has been set up.

Besides, an executive committee will be set up for suggesting ways and means for translating those specific objectives already formulated by the advisory committee.

The executive committee will include noted educationists in various State Organisations. Heads of the Institutions, and experts in the area of peace education.

The specific objectives tentatively set would be to:

1. Encourage peace-studies in India by setting up a clearing house of information in specific areas and providing guidelines for research on various issues.
2. Creating a forum for exchange of ideas in peace education by organising study circles seminars etc.
3. Setting up channels and mass media for dissemination of information on various cultures, lands and people.
4. Setting up a model child development institute for experimentation on the techniques of installing and generating peace and international understanding.
5. Publishing a News bulletin and quarterly dedicated to Peace Education.

The journal will be in the form of a quarterly with an editorial Board. Papers will be invited on different issues from people involved in peace research and relevant studies.

"At the time, when the world seems to have lost its reason, it seemed essential to give our *Children* the opportunity of considering *Peace*" as an issue which is relevant to them.

We can hardly afford the luxury of treating childhood as a time for play.

It is our aim to teach them to assume responsibility for their future, to preserve the natural beauty of their own surroundings and to establish values of friendship, tolerance, compassion and harmony as a way of living. It is then the time to learn:

(a) To communicate with the rest of the world.

(b) To live side by side in a spirit of friendship and respect for others, regardless of colour, customs or language.

(c) To increase the Sensitivity to beauty truth and goodness from early childhood and understanding.

Thus, basic concept of peace and harmony has to be instilled in the mind of the children in their own way:

Example

* Peace is when we all love one another because we are all the same.
* Peace is friendship — when nobody fights.
* Peace is light—peace is happiness.

UNESCO Circular No. 42 (1981) — International Understanding at School p. 29.

It is one of the goals to build-up a Peace movement, in the Young generation.